MW00790833

Writers on the criticism of Charles Williams

His literary criticism is valuable for its own sake, and helps us with his other work.

T. S. Eliot

He is best known by his criticism. I have learned much from it.

C. S. Lewis

It is precisely this power of evoking a very present and demanding life from that which might be supposed decently dead and sterilized, that characterizes all Charles Williams's literary criticism . . . It is not a scholarly approach at all, and it is not the kind of thing that has any real place in a "history of literature". It is a poet's approach: creative, vital, existential, seminal, timeless—and therefore, in a sense, without perspective.

Dorothy L. Sayers

I had met many good people before who made me feel ashamed of my own shortcomings, but in the presence of this man—we never discussed anything but literary business—I did not feel ashamed. I felt transformed into a person who was incapable of doing or thinking anything base or unloving.

W. H. Auden

Williams was a good theologian and, at his best, a great critic both formally and informally of English poetry because he recognized that language is arbitrary, autonomous, at the same time that it is bound, helpless.

Geoffrey Hill

A deeply serious critic, a poet unafraid of major risks, and a theologian of rare creativity.

He's someone who's chaotic, sometimes pretentious, sometimes waffly, sometimes unbearably clotted, and yet in the middle of it, there are so many gems.

Rowan Williams

THE
CELIAN
MOMENT
AND OTHER
ESSAYS

APOCRYPHILE
PRESS

THE
CELIAN
MOMENT
AND
OTHER ESSAYS

CHARLES WILLIAMS

EDITED BY
STEPHEN BARBER

Apocryphile Press
PO Box 255
Hannacroix, NY 12087
www.apocryphilepress.com

First published in Great Britain by The Greystones Press in 2017.
This new edition published by Apocryphile Press in 2024.
The selection, Introduction and Notes © Stephen Barber 2017.
Charles Williams's works are now public domain except as listed at
the end of the Sources and Acknowledgements.
Designed and typeset by Nigel Hazle.

Printed in the United States of America.
ISBN 978-1-958061-73-2 | paper
ISBN 978-1-958061-74-9 | ePub

No part of this book may be reproduced, stored in a retrieval system, or transmitted in
any form or by any means electronic, mechanical, photocopy, recording, or otherwise
without written permission of the author and publisher, except for brief quotations in
printed reviews.

Please join our mailing list at www.apocryphilepress.com/free
We'll keep you up-to-date on all our new releases,
and we'll also send you a FREE BOOK.
Visit us today!

Contents

Introduction

Charles Williams saw himself primarily as a poet but he earned his living as a versatile man of letters. As well as carrying out his day job as an editor for the Oxford University Press in their London office he also lectured at evening classes and wrote novels, biographies, plays, religious essays—and a good deal of literary criticism. There are several books and also a large number of essays, introductions and reviews. Anne Ridler collected some of them in *The Image of the City* and here is another gathering. All shed light not only on their subjects but also on Williams himself and together they give an overview of most of his literary enthusiasms.

The collection begins with two general essays. The first appeared as the introduction to an anthology of critical essays which is announced on the title page as 'selected and with an introduction by Phyllis M. Jones'. Although she is credited with editing other anthologies as well, the selection of essays here and the introduction bear all the marks of Williams and are consistent with the rest of his work. It seems that he ghosted this for her and publicly gave her the credit. He had done this once before, in a book credited to his wife. Phyllis

Jones was a younger colleague of his at the Oxford University
Press and his second love. The story of their long, tormented
and unconsummated relationship has recently been told in
Grevel Lindop's biography of Williams.[1]

There was a good deal of discussion at the time about the
function of criticism and T. S. Eliot's essay with that title was
widely discussed. In it he suggested that the task of criticism was
'the elucidation of works of art and the correction of taste' and
argued for what he called 'classicism' as opposed to 'the inner
voice'.[2] Williams in contrast offers three tasks for the critic;
the first two are not very different from Eliot's but to them he
adds: 'most important of all, he brings about some kind of unity
between the experiences which we connect with Life and those
we associate with Literature'. Unlike some of Eliot's academic
followers, Williams was always willing to make connections
from literature to philosophical or theological issues and indeed
at times seems to regard poetry as a secondary revelation with
almost scriptural authority. He develops this towards the end
of the essay, arguing that literature 'is a world which, to those
who choose to know it, is more real and more substantial than
the world of perceptible objects in which we move' and goes on
to ask rhetorically: 'Who has not walked down a street and felt
that the houses, the pavements themselves, were unreal?' and
continues with a magnificent statement of his *credo*: 'there is
nothing in this life which more arouses in our souls a knowledge
of their origin and their nature than the contemplation of
poetry.' I have taken the title 'The office of criticism' from the
closing phrase of this essay.

The title essay was written as the Introduction to *The New Book
of English Verse*, an anthology commissioned by the publisher

1   Grevel Lindop, *Charles Williams: The Third Inkling*, Oxford 2015.
2   T. S. Eliot, 'The Function of Criticism' in *Selected Essays*, London
    1951 (1932), 24, 27. This essay was first published in 1923.

Victor Gollancz. In it Williams ranges across English poetry from Chaucer to the Victorians Matthew Arnold and Gerard Hopkins; more recent poets were presumably unavailable to him for copyright reasons. Of particular interest is the concept of the 'Celian moment' which he puts forward, and which I have used as the title of this essay and of the collection.

> The Celian moment (so to call it) had a double vocation—as love and as poetry—and retains for us a passion in both. It is the moment which contains, almost equally, the actual and the potential; it is perfect within its own limitations of subject or method, and its perfection relates it to greater things.

This phrase, like Pound's 'image', Joyce's 'epiphany' or Eliot's 'objective correlative' represents something dear to the modernist writers of the twentieth century, in which the matter presented to us—whether in the world or in writing is immaterial—through the intensity of its expression presents also something beyond itself.

Williams is not normally thought of as a modernist but we find him here beginning to articulate the poetics behind his Taliessin sequence of poems, which he was writing at the time. He is also harking back to a much older tradition of symbolism, one which goes back through the medievals to Plato. Williams had already shown his familiarity with this line of thought in the novel *The Place of the Lion*, 1931, in which the Platonic ideas of various animals break through into the supposedly 'real' world of our everyday life.

In the year after this essay, C. S. Lewis described the fundamental idea:

> If our passions, being immaterial, can be copied by material inventions, then it is possible that our material world in its turn is the copy of an invisible world. As the god Amor and his figurative garden are to the actual passions of men, so perhaps we ourselves

and our "real" world are to something else. The attempt to read that something else through its sensible imitations, to see the archetype in the copy, is what I mean by symbolism or sacramentalism.[3]

A few years later Williams was to articulate the idea more directly in his own words by paraphrasing Coleridge to define what he meant by a symbol: 'a symbol must have three characteristics (i) it must exist in itself, (ii) it must derive from something greater than itself, (iii) it must represent in itself that greatness from which it derives'.[4]

Nevertheless we can note a certain nervousness in Williams in bringing out this idea. The apologetic phrase 'so to call it' suggests this, as also does the fact that he surrounds it with a dense thicket of references and allusions, like the sleeping beauty of the fairy tale. This is in fact the most allusive passage in any essay in this book. The reason for this defensiveness is that Celia was his pet name for Phyllis Jones. In taking up the phrase 'the Celian moment' to account for his own poetics he is both concealing and revealing his devotion to her.

The name Celia itself came from Marvell's 'The Match', a poem which he included in the anthology. The conceit in this poem is that nature laid up a treasure of all her perfections and these were combined in Celia. One spark ignited this:

> Thus all his fuel did unite
> To make one fire high:

3   Lewis, *The Allegory of Love*, Oxford 1936, 45. The exchange of letters between Lewis and Williams over this book, then being prepared for the press by Williams, and Williams's *The Place of the Lion*, which Lewis had just read, led to their friendship. I quote from this exchange below.

4   *The Figure of Beatrice*, London 1943, 7, paraphrasing Coleridge, *The Statesman's Manual*, London 1816, 36–7, also in *Collected Works*, Vol VI, *Lay Sermons*, Princeton 1972, 30.

Introduction

> None ever burned so hot, so bright:
> And Celia that am I.

The clue to the flurry of cryptic literary references is that they nearly all refer to poets who also made use of the name Celia, either to idealize a woman, or, as in the case of Swift and Pope, to satirise one. The most significant of these is that to Shelley, whose *Epipsychidion* addresses a young Italian woman in terms so idealized as practically to deify her:

> Seraph of Heaven! too gentle to be human,
> Veiling beneath that radiant form of Woman
> All that is insupportable in thee
> Of light, and love, and immortality!
> Sweet Benediction in the eternal Curse!
> Veiled glory of this lampless Universe!
> Thou Moon beyond the clouds! Thou living Form
> Among the Dead! Thou Star above the Storm!
> *Epipsychidion*, 21–8

There is a great deal more in the same vein. Williams wrote to, and about, Phyllis Jones, a large body of private poems praising her in very similar terms. Shelley prefaces his poem with a number of Dantean references, and Williams's full realization of his theory of love was to come to fruition in his conception of Beatrice of which there is a foretaste in *Religion and Love in Dante* included here.

In this context it is salutary to note C. S. Lewis's criticism of *Epipsychidion*, and therefore of this whole kind of idealizing love:

I think the thought implied in [*Epipsychidion*] a dangerous delusion. In it Shelley is trying to stand on a particular rung of the Platonic ladder, and I happen to believe firmly that that particular rung does not exist, and that the man who thinks he is standing on it is not standing but falling ... There is an element of spiritual, and also of carnal, passion in it, each expressed with great energy and sensibility, and the whole is marred, but not completely, by the false mode . . . in which the poet tries to blend them.[5]

This criticism of Shelley is also implicitly a criticism of Williams. And it comes with the more force from the man whose friendship with Williams began over Lewis's study of precisely this kind of love, the courtly love which was the subject of his *The Allegory of Love*, and who later sympathetically expounded Williams's use of what he called Beatricean vision in the Taliessin poems. Williams had written to Lewis: 'I regard your book as practically the only one I have ever come across, since Dante, that shows the slightest understanding of what this very peculiar identity of love and religion means'. In his reply Lewis repudiated the idea that he might have accepted this himself, saying: 'I think you will find that I nowhere commit myself to a definite approval of this blend of erotic and religious feeling'.[6] I wonder whether this paragraph preserves a record of a discussion Lewis and Williams might have had about idealization in love. Indeed, Lewis continued to brood over this issue until, many years later and after the experience of marriage, he wrote at length about Eros, concluding that: 'Eros, honoured without reservation and obeyed unconditionally, becomes a demon'.[7]

After these two general essays, all but one of the remainder deal with writers who were important to Williams. I have arranged them in chronological order of subject. The essay

5 C. S. Lewis, 'Shelley, Dryden and Mr Eliot', in *Selected Literary Essays*, Cambridge 1969, 203. This essay was first published in 1939.

6 Williams, letter to Lewis, 12 March 1936; Lewis, letter to Williams, 23 March 1936, in Lindop, *Charles Williams: The Third Inkling*, 256, 259.

7 Lewis, *The Four Loves*, London 1960, 127.

on Virgil was the introduction to a retelling of the *Aeneid*.
Williams valued Virgil in two ways: as the poet of the *Aeneid*
he presented the trials of Aeneas in the work of founding what
would eventually be Rome. Rome was, in Virgil's vision—he
knew very well that the reality was different—an example of
what Williams called the City, an ideal community of mutual
help and forbearance, almost equivalent to what Jesus meant
by the Kingdom and certainly the place of what Williams
later came to call Exchange. Furthermore, the historical Virgil
was recreated as a fictional character by Dante as his guide
to Hell and Purgatory. Williams does not discuss that here
but the paradox of the poet who was considered to prophesy
Christ in his fourth eclogue being excluded as a pagan from
the Christian heaven was a real one to him, as indeed it was
to Dante himself, and was only finally resolved for him in his
poem 'Taliessin on the death of Virgil' in *Taliessin through
Logres*. Williams also writes finely on Virgil's romanticism as
shown by his feeling for an anthropomorphised Nature, for
example in his river gods and sea nymphs. I have deleted a few
phrases referring to his occasional use of Dryden's translation.

The immediate stimulus to writing *Religion and Love in Dante*,
published as a pamphlet in 1940, seems to have been Denis
de Rougemont's *Passion and Society*.[8] Williams reviewed this
sympathetically but critically. He summed up de Rougemont's
view of passionate love as one that 'looks forward to suffering,
a death-desire, "the active passion of Night"'. Williams rejects
this and says:

> The great tradition of romantic love—renewed like the phoenix
> in every generation—is quite other than the desire of death.
> The passion-myth is a heresy of it: at moments a temptation; in

8   Denis de Rougemont, *Passion and Society*, translated Montgomery
    Belgion, London 1940 (French original 1939). There was a second
    edition, London 1956.

moments of agony a very great temptation. The grand pattern of the real glory takes long to explore, and involves many opposite experiences, including boredom. It too, as in Dante, leads to politics and the City.[9]

The subtitle of Williams's pamphlet is *The Theology of Romantic Love* and he takes the opportunity to give a sketch of how he sees the significance of Beatrice to Dante, and, by implication, of anyone beloved to their lover. In Beatrice Dante saw a revelation of divine glory: he saw her as if she were unfallen, even though in this life she, like him, was a fallen human being. This then imposes on him a discipline: 'could he indeed become the Glory which he saw and by which for a moment he had been transfused? . . . Dante has to become the thing he has seen. He has to become, by his own will, the *caritas* which was, by God's will, awakened in him at the smile of Beatrice; he has to be faithful to that great communication in the days when Beatrice does not smile.' Readers will need to decide whether this version of idealized love is free from the criticisms which Lewis brought to bear on courtly love and Shelley. Williams later worked out his thinking about this in detail in *The Figure of Beatrice*, perhaps his finest prose work. However, this shorter account has a continuing value, particularly in the detailed references to passages in the *Paradiso*, which Williams rather skimped in the later book.

The essay on *Henry V* is a pendant to the longer discussion of Shakespeare in *The English Poetic Mind*. It is an isolated piece, although the use of the word 'therefore' in its first sentence suggests that it might have been taken from a larger undertaking. His main interest is in the strange calm which comes over Henry before the battle of Agincourt, at a time when the English army's position looked hopeless:

9 Williams, *The Image of the City*, Oxford 1958, 161. Williams's review was first published in 1940.

'Tis good for men to love their present pains
Upon example; so the spirit is eas'd:
And when the mind is quicken'd, out of doubt,
The organs, though defunct and dead before,
Break up their drowsy grave, and newly move
With casted slough and fresh legerity.

Williams comments: 'He has rather more than accepted darkness, danger, defeat and death, and loves them. It is this which gives him a new quickening of the mind, new motions of the organs; it destroys sloth and the drowsy grave of usual life.' He once told his first biographer 'At bottom a darkness has always haunted me,'[10] and his admiration for Shakespeare's *Henry V* came because he saw in him someone who had faced such a darkness and found a way through it. It is very characteristic of Williams to treat Shakespeare as a spiritual teacher,[11] to focus on the state of a character's soul, and in particular on a character who might seem unpromising material for such a reflection.

Hubert Foss, Williams's colleague at the Oxford University Press and Head of the Music Department, also ran a private press, the Sylvan Press. He wanted to publish an edition of Webster's *The Duchess of Malfi* and asked Williams to write an introduction to it. It was to be illustrated by Michael Ayrton. Williams was pleased by the commission; he wrote to his wife: 'I should like to do that really well; after poetry, criticism is my real work'.[12] His enthusiasm for the commission was somewhat

---

10 Alice Mary Hadfield, *Charles Williams: An Exploration of His Life and Work*, Oxford 1983, 213.

11 He included a chapter on 'Forgiveness in Shakespeare' in his theological work *The Forgiveness of Sins*, London 1942, also included in *He Came Down from Heaven*, 1950 edition.

12 Williams, *To Michal from Serge: Letters from Charles Williams to His Wife, Florence, 1939–1945*, ed. Roma A. King, Jr., Kent and London 2002, 223.

dampened when Foss asked him to revise his essay as George Rylands, who was to contribute an essay on the production, had also written on the poetry.[13] Though he makes some telling points about the imagery of dung, earth and corruption, in fact the essay as we have it is less about the poetry than about the motivation of the characters. Williams takes a phrase from Middleton: 'You are the deed's creature' and uses it to examine the motivation of the duchess, her two murderous brothers, her husband Antonio and the repentant melancholic villain Bosola. He also defends the integrity of the play as a whole; many people have felt that it deteriorates after the death of the duchess—I have heard it described as descending from tragedy to melodrama. Williams particularly praises the echo scene in the fifth act where Antonio and Delio hear an echo from the duchess's grave with a voice like hers. Williams comments:

> This is perhaps the most purely moving scene which the Duchess has. Her earthly greatness has ended—royalty and courage alike. She is not even required to make another entry as a ghost. Webster would not so enliven death; it would have too much broken up his bloody and again corrupting earth.

The essay on Hopkins was the introduction to the second edition of his poems, published in 1930. The first edition had been edited by Hopkins's friend, the poet and later poet-laureate Robert Bridges, in 1918. When the time came for a new edition Bridges declined to handle it, being then preoccupied with his *magnum opus*, *The Testament of Beauty*, so the duty of preparing the new edition came to Williams. Williams added further poems which had come to light but also added his new introduction, which was much more positive than that of Bridges. It was thanks to this edition that Hopkins became so influential on the thirties poets, W. H. Auden and his generation. It was repeatedly reprinted and only replaced, after Williams's death, in 1948. It was aided on its

13 *To Michal from Serge*, 239.

way by the very tendentious inclusion of Hopkins as a modern poet by F. R. Leavis in his *New Bearings in English Poetry* of 1932, though his commendation did not extend to Williams's introduction, because Williams compared Hopkins to Milton.

After a brief reference to Hopkins's prosodic innovations Williams concentrates on his diction: his alliteration, compound nouns, interior rhymes and repetitions. But this diction comes from a 'simultaneous consciousness of a controlled universe, and yet of division, conflict, and crises within that universe'. It is for this divided sensibility that Williams compares Hopkins to Milton, not, as Leavis implies, for his diction. This awareness of division is a central theme in Williams's criticism: it appears again in the 'interior crisis' which he finds in *Troilus and Cressida* in *The English Poetic Mind*: 'that in which every nerve of the body, every consciousness of the mind, shrieks that something cannot be. Only it is.'[14] And at the end of his life it appears in his concept of the Impossibility: 'something that could not be, and yet was'.[15] Hopkins's diction also influenced him in his writing of the Taliessin poems, which are markedly different in style from his earlier poems and use many of the devices he examines in this essay.[16]

Williams's interest in Yeats was of long standing. His very first book, the sonnet sequence *The Silver Stair*, featured an epigraph from Yeats's *The Shadowy Waters*, and he gave him detailed and sympathetic treatment in his first critical book, *Poetry at Present*. He was particularly interested in Yeats's use of myth and magic and he would of course have known that Yeats had been an enthusiastic member of the magical society the Order of the Golden Dawn, and that he drew on magic as

14 *The English Poetic Mind*, Oxford 1932, 59ff..

15 Introduction to *Letters of Evelyn Underhill*, London 1943, 15.

16 There is a detailed discussion of this by Anne Ridler in her introduction to *The Image of the City*.

well as on mythology in his poetry. Williams himself had been a member of a successor order and he was also preoccupied with embodying myth in poetry, in his case Arthurian rather than Celtic. In the earlier book he praised the first edition of Yeats's *A Vision*, which, considering that it was published only in a limited edition of 600 copies and must have been hard to get hold of, shows that his interest in him was deep. It is not surprising that he should take the opportunity to review Yeats's later thorough revision of this book. He also seizes on the sentence which Yeats quotes from the pre-Socratic philosopher Heraclitus: 'dying each other's life, living each other's death'. He uses this to illustrate his own teaching about Exchange, one of the central concepts of his mature thought:

> If indeed the world is founded on an interchange so profound that we have not begun to glimpse it, such sentences for a moment illuminate the abyss.

This review was not the place to demonstrate it, but Williams had also taken up this phrase in his own poetry.[17] Williams's debt to Yeats as a thinker as well as a poet deserves more detailed treatment. It is pleasant to know that Yeats was pleased with this review, writing: '[Williams] is the only reviewer who has seen what he calls "the greatness and terror" of the diagram'.[18]

17 *Bors to Elayne: on the King's Coins*, 88, in *Taliessin through Logres*, for which he gives an acknowledgement to Yeats in his notes. He used it again in *The Last Voyage*, 74, and in *The Founding of the Company*, 64, in *The Region of the Summer Stars and in two of his plays, The Death of Good Fortune* and *The House of the Octopus, Collected Plays*, Oxford, 1963, 189 and 310. I have discussed this debt in more detail in 'Heraclitus and the way of exchange', *Charles Williams Society Newsletter*, No. 112, Autumn 2004.

18 Letter to Edith Shackleton Heald, 10 December 1937, quoted by Roy Foster, *W. B. Yeats: A Life II The Arch-Poet*, Oxford 2003, 607.

Yeats was an admired master of the older generation; Eliot was a slightly younger and very much more successful rival. He was also a friend of Williams, a situation which Williams negotiated with as much tact as he could. There was nevertheless an unease, which may account for the slight archness of the essay on *Four Quartets* and Williams's choice of putting it in the form of a dramatic dialogue. Of the names of the four dramatic characters I cannot explain Eugenio and Nicobar; Sophonisba comes from a play, while Celia was of course the name of Williams's second love, smuggled in, I suspect, for his private delectation.[19] She certainly seems to be speaking for Williams when she praises most the incantatory passages in Eliot, and Williams wrote similar incantatory passages in his Taliessin poems. However, the most important point in the review is the suggestion of Eugenio that, 'Few poets have been able to go all their distance; in any who have won to an end, and not to a mere breaking-off, we may be aware that there is but one thing said . . . [Eliot] is one who will have gone, it seems, all his distance.' This was an important concept for Williams, worked out in detail in *The English Poetic Mind*, where he says, for example, about Wordsworth, whom he greatly admired, that 'he missed the final wrestling'.[20] He later says that the 'one thing' for Eliot is that 'that you can only be a thing by becoming it'. This is reminiscent of what he said about Dante: 'Dante has to become the thing he has seen' so that this is a preoccupation of Williams at least as much as it might be for Eliot. Eugenio's later pronouncement, that 'The grace of time is to turn time into grace', with quotations from *Burnt Norton* and *The Dry Salvages*, is another point where they touch as poets, and I have quoted a passage from *Taliessin through Logres* which seems to me to provide a parallel from Williams's own poetry.

19 I have wondered whether Eliot's choice of the name Celia for the heroine of *The Cocktail Party*, might owe something to private conversations between Williams and Eliot.

20 *The English Poetic Mind*, 163.

'Ourselves and the Revolution' differs from all the other essays here in not being about literature but the political situation, specifically Hitler's invasion of Russia in 1941, which turned Russia into an ally and forced a re-examination of British attitudes to the Russian revolution. Williams cuts through political argument to point out that 'one thing it did seem to mean was the insistence on the desirability of a full stomach'. He goes on to say 'no one who has not had that experience ought to be allowed, in social articles, to use the word "insecurity." Insecurity means that you do not know how you are to pay for food and shelter, either for yourself or your family. It is, outside extreme physical pain, the worst experience of man; broken hearts are nothing to it.' Williams did not publicly take up a political stance though various scattered references have led Grevel Lindop to conclude that 'he was the only left-wing Inkling'.[21] But here we have the clearest possible statement that he was not a detached intellectual interested only in literature and theology and out of touch with the concerns of ordinary people. He was, indeed, regularly hard up, and at one time even said that he wrote all his books simply to support his son.[22] He also brought his sympathy for the revolution to his poetry: in 'The Calling of Arthur', King Cradlemas has 'tears for the poor' but no help and the people 'draw up the hammer and sickle', the flag of the post-revolutionary Soviet Union. Williams's willingness to accept an anachronism to make his point speaks for itself.

I have endeavoured to present the essays in the style which Williams would have wished for, if he had collected them himself. Indeed, he had thoughts in 1935 of doing so. Grevel Lindop informed me that in 1935 Williams had himself thought of writing or collecting a book of literary essays with the title *The Celian Moment* but that Kenneth Sisam, then

21 *Charles Williams, The Third Inkling*, xii.
22 Op. cit. 212.

Assistant Secretary to the delegates of the Oxford University Press, had been discouraging. I was delighted to find that he had projected the same title that I had independently already settled on. However, we do not know which essays he had in mind—apart presumably from the title essay here—and several of those I have chosen come from later than 1935.

Williams was an allusive writer and he quoted frequently from his well-stocked mind. However, he was not a scholar and he made little use of footnotes. Sometimes he worked some references into the text, as in the Virgil and Hopkins essays but more commonly he made quotations without references. He flatters the reader by implying that he or she has as wide a literary background as he had. In the particularly allusive paragraph of the title essay I mentioned above he throws out eight references to the names of women in pastoral or love poetry without identifying any of them and follows this with a plethora of allusions to poems whose most common feature is the use of the name Celia. I dare say many readers will recognize 'the Abyssinian maid', but not know which poems of Swift and Pope he is referring to—the latter possibly spurious—or even have heard of William Percy. I have decided to source all quotations and reference all allusions of this kind, though to keep down the number of notes I have grouped some together and put references after quotations where these are set off. Where he placed references in the text I have replaced these with notes and I have also replaced poem or page numbers with titles, first lines or line references as necessary so that they can be used, as far as possible, with any edition of the work he is quoting. Where he gave references in footnotes I have tidied these up. In the case of the Virgil and Dante essays I have given references to lines in the Latin and Italian originals and to the traditional section divisions of the *Vita Nuova*; these are keyed in most English translations. With Shakespeare and other playwrights remember that line references vary among editions, particularly in prose passages. There seemed no reason to interfere with his use of old-spelling texts in the essay on *The Duchess of Malfi*. I have given line references for longer poems but not for short ones. For prose I have tended to refer to book and chapter only, as pagination varies greatly among editions.

Williams belonged to a generation when Anglican Christians were brought up on the King James Bible and the 1662 *Book of Common Prayer* and he frequently alluded to them. Since these are nowadays less well known I have provided references where these explain the wording Williams chose.

Williams often quoted from memory and made occasional slips; I believe the writer who said 'Accuracy is fruitfulness— it is the first law of the spiritual life'[23] would have wanted these corrected. They are normally inconsequential and I have silently substituted the standard text, though I have usually left his punctuation; I have also corrected one or two dates. Where his slip might be of interest I have left it in the text or mentioned it in the note. All notes are by the editor except for the small number to which I have added the initials CW. I have occasionally supplemented these, either in square brackets within his text or with my own note. In a few places I have deleted a few sentences which refer to other parts of anthologies or collections not reprinted here.

Stephen Barber

NOTE FOR THE 2024 EDITION
This book was first published in 2017 and a corrected reprint followed in 2019. For this new edition I have made a few further corrections and revisions.

---

23 *The Figure of Beatrice*, 155.

Sources and Acknowledgements

'The office of criticism' was the introduction to *English Critical Essays: Twentieth Century*, noted as 'selected with an introduction by Phyllis M. Jones', London, OUP, 1933. Although it appeared over the name of Phyllis Jones, it is clearly the work of Williams. I am grateful to Roderick McDougall, son of the late Phyllis (Jones) McDougall, for permission to include this essay.

'The Celian moment' was the introduction to *The New Book of English Verse*, edited by Charles Williams, London, Gollancz, 1935. Lord David Cecil, Ernest de Selincourt and E. M. W. Tillyard are listed as Associate Editors.

'The story of the *Aeneid*' was the introduction to a retelling by Williams of Virgil's poem under that title, London, OUP, 1936.

'Religion and Love in Dante: The Theology of Romantic Love' was published as a pamphlet by the Dacre Press, London, 1941.

'Shakespeare's *Henry V*' was written for *Shakespeare Criticism 1919-1935*, edited by Anne Bradby (later Ridler), London, OUP, 1936.

'On the poetry of *The Duchess of Malfi*' was written as an introduction to a private press edition of Webster's play, London, the Sylvan Press, 1945.

'The poems of Gerard Manley Hopkins' was the 'Introduction to the second edition' under that title, London, OUP, 1930. I have deleted the opening section, which was specific to that edition and separated from the main discussion.

'Staring at miracle: *A Vision* by W. B. Yeats' was a review in *Time and Tide*, 4 December 1937.

'*Four Quartets*: a dialogue on Mr Eliot's poem', originally titled simply 'A dialogue on Mr Eliot's poem', was a review in *Dublin Review* 212, April 1943. At this time the four poems had all been published individually but they were not collected under the overall title *Four Quartets* until 1944.

'Ourselves and the revolution' was an article in *Russia and the West*, edited by C. A. Dawson, London, 1942.

'The office of criticism' appeared over the name of Phyllis M. Jones, who was an employee of the Oxford University Press. The essays on Virgil, Shakespeare and Hopkins were written by Williams in his role as an editor for the Press. In all these cases Oxford University Press retain the copyright. These items appear by permission of the Secretary to the Delegates of Oxford University Press. I am grateful to Dr Martin Maw, archivist of OUP, for facilitating this. The other items remain in copyright in the USA and some other territories and are reprinted by permission.

Sources and Acknowledgements

I am grateful to friends and colleagues for their help with this project. Dr Brian Horne, the Revd Dr Richard Sturch and Emeritus Professor Grevel Lindop have provided advice on various points. Grevel Lindop also supplied a copy of 'Ourselves and the revolution', an article by Williams which he unearthed in the course of research for his indispensable biography of Williams, *Charles Williams: The Third Inkling* (Oxford 2015). He also gave me other information I have cited. Professor Valerie Rumbold provided information about the doubtful authenticity of a poem attributed to Pope. I am also grateful to the Charles Williams Society, now defunct, for expressing their support in the very tangible form of a grant, and to my sister, Dr Anna Baldwin, for doing the same.

1

The Office of Criticism

The impulse from which criticism arises is that which prompts the much-maligned man who says 'I know what I like'. But the critic as he becomes professional, as (that is) he professes his liking more and more publicly and officially, becomes evangelistic. To his ardent spirit the next step from knowing what he likes is the conviction that others ought to be converted to that preference: that here, in fact, is the true faith in Literature, and the sooner others realize it the sooner will they be saved, not from future damnation but from present embarrassment—the possession of an undesirable taste in literature. Sometimes the undesirable is also unfashionable, and to the fear of being unfashionable the contemporary critic owes in every age his happy dictatorship. He, unlike the modest user of the cliché, doesn't say that 'he doesn't know much about Literature' or Music or whatever: on the contrary, almost his first endeavour is to convince us as subtly as possible of the catholicity of his knowledge and the justice of his principles in order to prove his right to his chair of doctrine. Criticism then, on the lowest plane, might be said to be the effort of the individual mind to persuade the mass mind that his faith is that one most worthy of all men to be received.[1] And the reader is apt to feel at times that, like some other missionary spirits, the critic believes that the end justifies the sometimes tedious means. In so doing, the critic, if he succeeds at all, accomplishes one of three main things: (1) he instructs us in the accidents of his subject by elucidating obscure passages and references, by purifying the text, by deciding bibliographical details and in numerous other ways bringing order out of what was textual chaos; or (2) he acts as a guide to our emotions—those emotions, that is to say, which are aroused by art—classifying them according to their causes and deciding in the light of his own experience what particular quality of each work is responsible for each particular emotion; or (3) and most important of all, he brings about some kind of unity between the experiences which we connect with Life and those we associate with Literature. It is unnecessary to add that these three accomplishments are not exclusive—a critic may do one, two, or all three of them in the space of one essay.

Of the first two it is perhaps superfluous to try to assign the more important place. A long tradition, mostly and necessarily academic, attributes to the first an honourable if cloistered name; a name which, if it never receives the highest honours, is seldom discredited. True, Bentley[2] did alter

They hand in hand with wandering steps and slow,

1   'This is a true saying and worthy of all men to be received, that Jesus Christ came into the world to save sinners,' 1 Timothy 1: 15 as quoted in *Book of Common Prayer*, Holy Communion, Comfortable Words.

2   Richard Bentley (1662–1742), classical scholar. In 1732 he published an edition of Milton's *Paradise Lost* supposedly purged of errors introduced by others and rewritten by himself. It became notorious. (It is discussed in William Empson's *Some Versions of Pastoral*, 1935.) The quoted passage is the last two lines of the poem, with Bentley's proposed revision.

Through Eden took their solitary way

to

They, hand in hand with social steps their way
Through Eden took, with heavenly comforts cheered;

but we owe to Theobald

for his nose was as sharp as a pen, and a' babbled of green fields.[3]

The first you can take or leave as you like. Bentley liked it: we do not. But the second few will want to reject. It is constructive criticism at its best, taking something which was obviously nonsense and making not so much sense as inspiration. If the modern reader is sometimes apt to underrate the value of the textual critic it is probably because he has never had anything but a good text to read. Future generations may not find so much use for that kind of criticism. Good texts of even the worst authors are stored in all but indestructible security: contemporary critics of contemporary authors will have elucidated all the obscure references long before the man is dead, let alone before time has proved him worth explaining. Elucidatory notes of this kind are like sauces; one takes them or one doesn't. If one does they are ready to hand; if one prefers the author unexplained and unaccompanied, he is always there. But even in the latter case you can hardly fail to honour the man who gives you your plain text as perfect as he can make it.

To the second class belong the majority of present-day critics. It includes a large body of writers, from the rare best to the

3   Lewis Theobald (1688–1744) produced an edition of Shakespeare in 1726 in which he emended Mistress Quickly's words on the death of Falstaff in *Henry V*, II. 3. 16 from 'a Table of green fields', the text of the First Folio, to 'a' babbled of green fields'. The emendation is almost universally accepted.

more frequent worst. The critic of this kind at his best is a guide to our sensitiveness. He knows that there are certain passions common to all men and that these can be worked on by certain qualities in art; the reader is not always aware of this—he may not even recognise the quality though he is conscious of the emotion: the critic will be his guide. For example—there is, in effect, says Mr Saintsbury, 'some quality of verse which we are agreed to call the "Grand Style"'[4]: the masters of this style are A, B. C, &c.; they bring it to perfection in the following quotations. When you read these phrases or passages you are under the influence of 'the perfection of expression in every direction and kind', and when this perfection works in such a way that it transports and transmutes the subject, then the 'Grand Style' exists. It may be the metre that is affecting you, or an evoked double or single image, or superb diction—or a hundred other causes. But when it exists its effect is infallible. It is true; only, when you have said that

She has been fairer, Madam, than she is,[5]

is in the Grand Style, and partly produces its effect by 'the double meaning' and 'pathetic moderation and modulation of

4   The definition by George Saintsbury (1845–1933) in his essay 'Shakespeare and the Grand Style' (1910) is: 'The perfection of expression in every direction and kind, the commonly called great and the commonly called small, the tragic and the comic, the serious, the ironic and even to some extent the trivial (not in the worst sense of course). Whenever this perfection of expression acquires such force that it transmutes the subject and transports the hearer or reader, then and there the Grand Style exists, for so long and in such a degree as the transmutation of the one and the transportation of the other lasts.' This essay was included in the volume to which this essay of Williams was the introduction.

5   *Two Gentlemen of Verona*, IV. 4. 145. The disguised Julia is speaking about herself to Sylvia, for whom her lover Proteus has deserted her.

the disguised and deserted mistress'[6] you still don't know what it is that is the essence of the effect, except that it can be labelled the 'Grand Style', and there you are back at the beginning, deeply grateful to Mr. Saintsbury for having carried you thus far, but with the unsatisfied feeling that all has not yet been explained, and that the secret lies deeper, only to be come at by prayer and fasting and long hours of watching, not with the critics, but with the poets themselves. The emotion we know: a similar acute experience (not necessarily an identical one) can be aroused by the line of the Wiltshire Downs, by a Bach aria, by a Renoir painting—each a perfection of expression. But what is there peculiar to an arrangement of words, more especially to poetry, that it can produce an emotion as deep as any that life has to offer? (It has been thought convenient here to except in all cases man's relation to God, which may or may not be so very different from his relation to Letters, more particularly to poetry, save that for Letters some native inborn desire may or may not exist, but for the former we must believe that a native inborn desire does exist.)

Criticism as a tradition in England might be thought to have begun and ended with Arnold: before him was splendid chaos, after him the overwhelming flood. Up to and including Arnold criticism in England was concerned with assessing and discovering certain values which it considered to be important, but which varied from time to time. It may have misjudged them; in some cases it certainly over-estimated them: but what they were in each century it certainly knew—even when the value sunk as low as mere conventional morality. Modern criticism has no hierarchy among the qualities it seeks—if indeed it seeks any qualities at all; it appears to know as little what it wants from Letters as the modern generation does of what it wants from Life. The finest effects of the traditional

6   Both these phrases are also from Saintsbury's essay and refer to Julia.

critics—say of Johnson or Lamb—were to a large extent brought about by the production in the reader of an equivalent emotion. The most popular, and one of the finest, examples is De Quincey's essay *On the Knocking at the Gate in* Macbeth. A similar effect is in Johnson's sentence on the same play: 'He that peruses Shakespeare looks round alarmed and starts to find himself alone.'[7] This kind of writing communicates by its own style the virtue it is engaged in assessing. We think that Johnson was very often wrong about Shakespeare: we are quite certain he was wrong about Lycidas;[8] and yet there is in that wrongness something which is nearer to Shakespeare and Milton than many more correct estimates of these poets will ever be. You may learn nothing from him or Arnold (though usually you may learn much), but you will get a reflection of what you felt when you read the original. You will know that reflection, and the original image will be reduplicated in your mind.

The present chaotic state of criticism has been enhanced by several accidental things. No period has ever been so free from a prejudice against any of the past as our own; we do not object to Elizabethans or Augustans, Romantics or Victorians—we enjoy them all. It is much to our good, but our catholicity has helped to abolish principles as well as prejudices. The chaos is enormously increased by the tacit assumption that reviewing is criticism. Reviewing may or may not be criticism, but when a reviewer states that 'this is the worst novel I have read for a long time' no one imagines that he has even begun to criticize—that he has done more than say 'I know what I like—and this is not it'. (That reviewing may be criticism

7 Samuel Johnson, 'Miscellaneous Observations on the Tragedy of *Macbeth*', 1745.

8 Johnson said of Milton's *Lycidas*: 'the diction is harsh, the rhymes uncertain, and the numbers unpleasing', *Lives of the Poets*, 'John Milton'.

it is hoped has been proved by the inclusion here[9] of some essays which originally appeared in that form.) Again writing has become the favourite form of self-expression; and of all forms of writing the essay critical, sown at school and fostered and watered in the Universities, is second only to the novel in commonness. To be a reviewer or a publisher's reader is the ideal and inward conceit of every young man or woman who was ever said to be good at Literature. That very few reviewers have even begun to know what they are looking for is quite obvious; but that is mostly a reflection of life. When a generation arises that knows quite surely what it is looking for in life so soon will it know what it wants in Literature; and just as soon, probably, will it get it.

The terms Life and Literature are usually used to denote separate experiences. But the significance of Literature is that it is not only a part of life, but a life itself and in some sense an equivalent of the greater one; 'the complementary life', as Alice Meynell called it.[10] To reconcile these three facts is the final task of the critic. 'Our destiny, our being's heart and home, Is with infinitude', says Wordsworth. It is with

> Effort, and expectation and desire
> And something evermore about to be.
> > *The Prelude* (1850 text), 604–608

If the mind of man is only capable of grasping finite things, yet its destiny, according to Wordsworth, is with something which it will never entirely apprehend. It is the true business of the critic, as of the poet, to make this apprehension as complete as possible, but his boundaries are more clearly marked; he

9   I.e. in the anthology to which this essay was the introduction.
10 Alice Meynell (1847–1922), poet and an early mentor to Williams. This phrase is from the introduction to her anthology *The Flower of the Mind* (1897).

has to bring about a unity of experience between what we call Life and what we distinguish in the great traditional word Letters—*orbis litterarum humaniorum.*[11] It is a world which, to those who choose to know it, is more real and more substantial than the world of perceptible objects in which we move. Who has not walked down a street and felt that the houses, the pavements themselves, were unreal? But who of any that have loved Milton has ever felt that

> Thus with the year
> Seasons return; but not to me returns
> Day, or the sweet approach of even or morn,
> Or sight of vernal bloom, or summer's rose,
> Or flocks, or herds, or human face divine
> *Paradise Lost*, III. 40–4

was anything but reality itself? Every storm we have ever known may pass from our recollection, but we remember every incident from the appearance of the 'very remarkable sky', in the storm that destroyed Steerforth.[12] A man may very well choose not to know, or to reject this world (just as surely as Satan chose Evil instead of Good[13]), but that is a matter of choice and not of knowledge. If a man knows anything of Shakespeare and others he will know that they have 'Voices more than all the winds with power'.[14] What that power is we shall almost certainly never know (unless perhaps by attending to that subject which this essay has excepted from its concern): it may be that the power itself lies in just that capacity to arouse in us a consciousness of 'something evermore about to be'; that, *exceptis excipiendis*,[15] there is nothing in this life which

11 'The world of humane letters', i.e. of literary studies.
12 Dickens, *David Copperfield*, Chapter 55.
13 'Evil be thou my Good', Milton, *Paradise Lost*, IV. 110.
14 Wordsworth, *The Prelude* (1850 text), V. 107.
15 With all necessary exceptions.

more arouses in our souls a knowledge of their origin and their nature than the contemplation of poetry. We know things first of all in life and we know them again more fully and more clearly in poetry: in poetry it is possible to know even pain and desolation—our own pain and desolation—as fruitful rather than sterile things. At the end of the *Prelude* Wordsworth, speaking of the purpose of the poets, says:

> Prophets of Nature, we to them will speak
> A lasting inspiration, sanctified
> By reason, blest by faith: what we have loved,
> Others will love, and we will teach them how;
> Instruct them how the mind of man becomes
> A thousand times more beautiful than the earth
> On which he dwells, above this frame of things
> (Which, 'mid all revolutions in the hopes
> And fears of men, doth still remain unchanged)
> In beauty exalted, as it is itself
> Of quality and fabric more divine.
>
> *The Prelude* (1850 text), XIV. 446–455
> (the close of the poem)

Would it be too much to say that, at its highest, this was the office of criticism?

2

The Celian Moment

The two roles laid down by the Publisher for this work[1] were (1) that it should contain nothing which was in the Oxford Book of English Verse[2] or the Golden Treasury,[3] (2) that every poem included should be of poetic importance. The first rule has been (it is hoped) strictly kept, except for one stanza of Chaucer. There are several editions of the Golden Treasury; I have worked on the Oxford edition. The degree to which the second rule has been kept will inevitably be disputed. But to say "of poetic importance" is not the same as to say "great poetry". There are poems here which have rather an indirect than a direct relation to greatness; it is hoped that there is none which is entirely without some relation. English poetry must not too sternly be confined to

1 *The New Book of English Verse*, London 1935. The publisher was Victor Gollancz.

2 This was the original *Oxford Book of English Verse*, edited by Arthur Quiller-Couch, 1900.

3 *The Golden Treasury of English Songs and Lyrics*, edited by Francis Turner Palgrave, first published 1861 and frequently revised. The Oxford edition Williams refers to is dated 1921.

immediate exaltations of the spirit; or rather, it must be allowed to find a sense of that delighted exaltation in pleasurable by-ways. An example is the Mistress Nicely of Hood's admirable sonnet ('She was a woman peerless in her station'). She is not Milton's Eve, but she retains and reflects in small an element in Milton's Eve, and Eve is, as it were, agreeably analyzed for us by that reflected figure, as the figure itself is accentuated by our knowledge of her greater kinswoman. A poetry which too intently included the housekeeper of Eden and rejected the housekeeper of Covent Garden would be a poetry unhealthily limited to its greatest moments. It is, of course, possible to object to Mistress Nicely that she represents an undesirable social order. So, for that matter, may Tamburlaine; and even some of Shakespeare's princes are not politically modern. There is a point, in many lesser poems, where poetic judgement and non-poetic judgement become involved. Upon the incidence of that point opinion will always differ, and the subject is too large to be discussed here. It need not for that reason be assumed that any of the editors[4] were unaware of it.

An accidental interest of my own (if a personal apology may be permitted) added a third direction to the two given above. I have sometimes, in making a choice preferred to include verse which contained a certain critical comment. The criticism of poetry by poetry is never quite the same as criticism in prose, and English poetry has always possessed a high capacity for reflecting, and reflecting on, itself. It has certainly done this by its mere complex existence, as in the case of Eve and Mistress Nicely; its very variations are criticism. But also it has ranged from direct adoration to direct parody and in parodying it has uttered criticism of poetic experience and created new experience. The great example of parody is Reynolds's *Peter*

---

4 Williams listed Lord David Cecil, Ernest de Selincourt and E. M. W. Tillyard as Associate Editors.

Bell;[5] too long to be given, impossible to cut, and almost too sublime an achievement to bear the name.

The difficulty of composing any anthology which covers more than a few years is the necessity which the reader as much as the compiler is under of continuously making (in Dr. Tillyard's phrase) a "fundamental readjustment of standards."[6] Both (*de nobis fabula*[7]), turning the pages of the old originals or of the new collection are apt unconsciously to apply the standards of (say) Spenser to Milton, to approve or disapprove on principles which are, in the strictest sense, "out of date." Certainly any mind adult in poetry should be superior to this, but certainly also every mind is much more likely to think itself, than to be, superior. There is hardly any limit to self-satisfaction and self-deception in the reading of poetry. It is not that we nowadays, we who think we read, are violently apt to prefer one period or one style to another. No; that mistake our century and our educated minds remove from us. If and as we prefer, we recognise and deprecate our idiosyncrasies. The error that remains is more subtle and more dangerous: we blur. We do not perhaps reject on or another standard, but we confuse them by carrying over. Contrast is deeply lost; the mere superficial instruction of our

5 John Hamilton Reynolds wrote a parody of Wordsworth's narrative poem *Peter Bell*.

6 I have not found this phrase in Tillyard's published works and it does not seem characteristic of him, though he might have said it in discussion. The source seems to be T. S Eliot: 'The existing order is complete before the new work arrives; for order to persist after the supervention of novelty, the *whole* existing order must be, if ever so slightly, altered; and so the relations, proportions, values of each work of art toward the whole are readjusted; and this is conformity between the old and the new.' 'Tradition and the Individual Talent', *The Sacred Wood*, London 1920, 50, and reprinted in *Selected Essays*, 15.

7 *De nobis fabula narratur*: about us is the story told. Latin tag adapted from Horace: *de te | fabula narratur*: the story is told about you, *Satires*, I. i. 69–70.

sensibilities continues to substitute an easy for a profound difference. To this error the great and memorable increase of scholarship has perhaps a little contributed. Scholarship as well as poetry has its camp followers: the recognition of similarities, the discovery of sources, the exhibition of borrowings, all of interest and sometimes of importance, have yet allowed the likeness, and not the difference, in the use of a line or a phrase to become the memorable thing. Rochester, writing

> Youth in her Looks, and Pleasure in her Bed,
> > 'A Letter from Artemisia in the Town to
> > Chloe in the Country', 196

and Gray writing

> Youth at the prow and Pleasure at the Helm,
> > 'The Bard: A Pindaric Ode', II. 2

are subtly discommoded into similarity, when in fact the difference is as broad as that between another line of Rochester's,

> 'Tis below wit, they tell you, to admire,
> > 'A Letter from Artemisia', 64

and Pope's

> For fools admire, but men of sense approve.
> > 'An Essay on Criticism', 391

Some effort to avoid this fault has been made in the present book by submitting various sections to those students of the grand art whose distinguished names illuminate a title-page else too pallid,[8] and by taking advice from others whose help is

---

8   I.e. the Associate Editors mentioned above, note 4.

acknowledged separately. There is perhaps no necessity here to particularise which name governs which period, since for one thing the final responsibility for all inclusions and exclusions is undoubtedly and entirely my own; for another, I have in certain instances discussed them with more than one of my courteous associates and others; for a third, it is not improper to leave undecided the exact weight of opinion behind any particular decision. It has been too often my own ungrateful office to exclude the exquisitenesses suggested by more informed minds; in a few places I have persisted in an inclusion which was generally deprecated.

In this matter of excision—since the first actual selection came to something like 1,200 pages, and even that had involved reluctant harshness—two questions arose: (1) did I at the last choice include a poem everyone certainly knew or a poem everyone perhaps did not know—or did not so well know? (2) did I retain a long poem or extract at the expense of omitting several short poems? I do not profess to have evolved or followed any principle in answer to either question. It will be quite easy for anyone to say he would rather have had no Chamberlayne and no Cartwright but more Donne and more Browning. It will be as easy to say that the *Anatomy of the World* or the *Prologue to the Satires* or *Nymphidia*[9] should have been farther reduced to make room for more Elizabethan songs or for more Romantic Lyrics. English poetry, however, does not consist chiefly of lyrics, nor is the poetry of long poems made up merely of lyric moments. The longer poems and extracts given are all examples of particular kinds of writing; and without some such examples the massive of poetry can hardly be approached. It might indeed well be argued that we should all do much better to attend to two or three long poems, and let the others be. But then we should be likely to become pedants rather than saints; poetry has to be counteracted by

9   By, respectively, Donne, Pope and Drayton.

itself. The answer therefore to both those questions has been determined by a kind of critical expediency, for excuse of which the most that can be hoped is a kindness in the reader.

There remain still the few—Shakespeare, Milton, Wordsworth, Chaucer. Keats fortunately had been more or less settled for me by Sir Arthur Quiller-Couch. He gave the Odes, and that, effectively, left *Hyperion*, and the preparation for the Odes. I have not attempted to give even a decent minority of the great passages in the great poets; the problem has been settled by other methods.

The effort to correct the inevitable prejudice of single minds by association of judgement is an effort to avoid Cant. Every anthology (unless of Cant) is, by its very nature, an attempt to avoid Cant, which is the great and everlasting enemy of Poetry, and, like other lasting enemies of the Good, all but omnipotent. A study of Cant in English poetry would be worth making. It is a matter for discussion whether, before about Marlowe's time, it existed at all. Monotony of verse existed, and religious and social cant no doubt existed in verse, but poetic cant needed print in order to grow. It needed wide communication of sensibility and intellect; the re-introduction of intellect in the time of Marlowe helped to give it its modern opportunity. Cant is a conscious thing, though naturally its dupes do not call it by its name; how should they? But the fresh discoveries of some sudden period are made, and almost before they have been realised the earnest traders and missionaries of verse are opening up the new lands. They say the new songs; they too often denigrate the old. The markets of Cant are set up, and a hitherto silent sea receives the chorus of his idolaters.

Cant indeed is a danger wherever, in the grand art anything appears but the most extreme poetic honesty it its moments of extreme poetic success; that is, much more, often than not. Even the great poets are subject to it though less than others, for they have in them a knack of introducing some other element at the same time, so that their cant is made either negligible or enjoyable Shakespeare does this with the Elizabethan rhetorical cant; he infuses into its wildness a laughter which keep intelligence alive. (It will probably be wise to add that I do not say Shakespeare did this deliberately; only that it is the result of his particular manner of writing.) Milton had more difficulty, for his intensity had two kind of Cant to deal with—poetic cant and religious cant, but he so managed his art as to make the very danger of them interesting. Indeed, he succeeded too well, for we have too long missed the simple fact that to Milton the whole Satanic rebellion was not only wicked but silly, and not only silly but comic.[10] He gave rise—how unintentionally!—to the cant of the Devil, while he was successfully transmuting the danger of cant about God. Thereby, certainly, he rounded the circle, and generations have piously restored to him the cant he laboured so well to throw away.

The more obvious conventions of the Augustans, the diction and rhythms by which among them the supreme courage of Pope dominated his sensibilities and purged his mind, were more quickly copied by the children of Cant; and for a long while indeed their whole age was supposed to be under its dominion. An age which at its greatest took hold of an extreme convention of language to conceal and control its pain was misunderstood, especially since it was immediately followed by an age which found a new diction to publish and proclaim its pain. Romanticism is now observed to exist all through the Augustans; it is in balance that we remark the Romantics falling into their own kind of cant. Shelley was perhaps in the greatest danger; the "aerial music"[11] has sometimes a dubiously,

---

10 Williams elaborates his view of Satan in *Paradise Lost* in *The English Poetic Mind*, Oxford 1932, 120–7.

11 'His finest passages have a witchery of aerial music, an exquisiteness of ideal beauty, and a white intensity of spiritual passion', W. J. Alexander, Introduction to Shelley, *Select Poems*, London 1898.

habitual sound about it. Keats was almost free. At the turn of the Nightingale Ode, in that unforgettable forest it lay in wait for him, and he avoided it, for he lost (he said in the very poem) the real music. It caught him for a moment in the last stanza of the *Urn*;[12] certainly there is poetic cant in the pretence that the figures in the urn are living, and though the last two lines may be true in some other state of being, they are not true there and so. Wordsworth is a more difficult problem; there is cant in him, but it is not so often poetic cant as intellectual, and it is often mixed with a dullness which is not quite the same thing. He put in a lot of things because he felt he ought; but it is not generally when things are put in that Cant appears. It is more usually when nothing is put in, or when much is left out.

Wordsworth, however, was only almost a Romantic, and it was in spite of him rather than by him that the cant of Nature in poetry escaped from the deliberate Augustans into the nineteenth century. We still in our ordinary lives linger a little in the decadence of Wordsworth, for the conventions of that age left minor poetry still inclined to attach a curious and unexplained importance to daffodils and such, and we remark their destruction with borrowed and uninvestigated grief. Wordsworth had advanced through daffodils to the skeleton in man's mind; it was that skeleton the shadow of which lay over the Victorians. A false and obtruded sensibility in our

12   O Attic shape! Fair attitude! with brede
        Of marble men and maidens overwrought,
     With forest branches and the trodden weed;
        Thou, silent form, dost tease us out of thought
     As doth eternity: Cold Pastoral!
        When old age shall this generation waste,
     Thou shalt remain, in midst of other woe
        Than ours, a friend to man, to whom thou say'st,
     'Beauty is truth, truth beauty,'—that is all
        Ye know on earth, and all ye need to know.
                    'Ode on a Grecian Urn', stanza V.

criticism has long made us curiously insensitive to the macabre which haunted them. We have turned them all, all those great nerve-stressed and moral-heartened creatures, into silhouettes of an optimism they achieved only, whenever they did achieve it, by sheer hard fighting. For example, we used to remember that Robert Browning made one of his characters sing,

> God's in His heaven—
> All's right with the world,
>
>> Pippa in *Pippa Passes*, I. 228–9

but we forget that, at the end of his greatest poem, he asserted that

>> our human speech is naught.
> Our human testimony false, our fame
> And human estimation words and wind.
>
>> *The Ring and the Book*, XII. 834–6

It is hoped that the poems and extracts given here may do a little to correct that injudiciousness. When they had a horror to control they did not cant; that came in with those who controlled no passion by their convention. Cant is neither mere dullness nor simple convention. A poet may be flat without cant, and may use the poetic ritual of his day without cant. The language of poetry is bound to be ceremonial, however direct. It is when versifiers (that is ceremonialists) use such a language without the intensity it should convey and concentrate that Cant begins to exist; it is when ceremony is willingly accepted as a substitute for intensity that it triumphs. The greatest moments of art are the moments, the only moments, when we can certainly know that ceremony and intensity exist at once; in daily life they are unapt to coincide. It is by the introduction of a new ceremonial method that a revolt against Cant begins—Augustan, Romantic, contemporary. Mathematics and machinery have provided us, in general, with a new ceremony, since Mr. Kipling wrote *McAndrew's Hymn*;

it is not their least service. So the ceremony of emotional logic is now substituted for intellectual, and our consciousness of poetry is again enlarged. The progress of poetry has been the continual discovery of a variation in ceremony to manifest some new intensity of the complex life of imagination, power always growing towards the "absolute power" of Wordsworth's definition in the *Prelude*[13] and of his other line "the two great ends of liberty and power."[14]

This changing ceremony has chronologically certain moments of clarity; it is remarkable in some of the early poems, in Skelton, in some Elizabethan lyrics, in the Restoration. Not even poetry, however, can restore us to the potentialities of the Middle Ages; with Marlowe our development went one way and not another, and since Marlowe there is a sense in which the clarity of Restoration lyric is the most potential; that is, it possesses more capacity than almost any later, or any greater poetry of becoming, in its development, one of several things. Chronologically we know what it did become. But as in time it lies between the Metaphysicals and the Augustans so in value it possesses something of the characteristics of both, and even of other periods. Rochester, for example, has in him something of several periods, and a full development of none. He was not so great a poet as either Donne or Pope, but he was nearer to both than they to each other. There was no such inclusive pause between the Augustans and the Romantics; Byron is a near example, but he was a later reaction from the Romantics, being always against the Government, in poetry as in politics. Nor

13   This spiritual Love acts not nor can exist
     Without Imagination, which, in truth,
     Is but another name for absolute power
     And clearest insight, amplitude of mind,
     And Reason in her most exalted mood.
                     The Prelude (1850 text), XIV. 188–192.
14   Wordsworth's line is actually 'To the great ends of liberty and power', *The Prelude* (1850 text), XII. 139.

was there any such between the Romantics and the Victorians. Beddoes offered a path, but Beddoes was almost the very name of that consciousness of horror against which the Victorians fought; the failure of *Death's Jest Book* was a symbolical failure. In a sense, it had its revenge; it made of its successors a Death's Jest Book, for its skeletons haunted them, and were neither quite raised into a new poetic heaven nor altogether exorcised from a moral serenity. Rochester loved the skeleton too much to be a Victorian, yet his verse, like theirs, desired the control of change. Change in him was chiefly change in love, as with other poets of his time; but in him peculiarly the intensity of his poetry's swift passage sometimes leaves us uncertain whether he is indeed speaking of fidelity or change. That Restoration moment, so hovering, attracted to itself the names of many femininities, and those names in the songs take on a kind of identity with the songs: Myra and Amaryllis, Chloe and Dianeme, Amoret, Stella, Ianthe, Celia.[15] The Celian moment (so to call it) had a double vocation—as love and as poetry—and retains for us a passion in both. It is the moment which contains, almost equally, the actual and the potential; it is perfect within its own limitations of subject or method, and its perfection relates it to greater things. It is the moment of passion, and it is described both for love and for poetry, in Marvell's Celian

15 These are names in pastoral and love poetry:
    Myra: Fulke Greville, *Caelica* sonnet sequence.
    Amaryllis: John Milton, *Lycidas*.
    Chloe: William Cartwright, 'To Chloe who for his sake wished herself younger'.
    Dianeme: Robert Herrick, 'To Dianeme'.
    Amoret: Robert Vaughan, 'To Amoret gone from him'.
    Stella: Philip Sidney, *Astrophil and Stella* sonnet sequence.
    Ianthe: Percy Bysshe Shelley, 'To Ianthe'; Ianthe was his daughter.
    Celia: Andrew Marvell, 'The Match'. Celia was also Williams's private name for Phyllis Jones, his second love, to whom he wrote many unpublished and uncollected poems.

poem, 'The Match'.[16] It had existed earlier in the unweighted lyricism of the early Elizabethans distinguishing the Celia of Jonson from her of William Percy; it is in the first comedies of Shakespeare and in the bruited Neaera of Cambridge. It was subjected later, as love and as poetry, to the exact comments of Swift and of Pope; it endured the illumination of Shelley and was transformed in Coleridge to Christabel and the Abyssinian maid and their world. With them it abandoned the Mall in which it had for a little time walked, and when it returned to the town in the full nineteenth century, it came, both in love and in poetry, to a limited greatness, for it had—with certain great exceptions—lost the secret of the overtones. It was still bright with something of angelic light, from "the top of speculation";[17] few then explored the angelhood.

But if by mere chronology Celia vanished, after so many songs had been unavailingly offered her, yet in poetry, as in love, she had already achieved a greater end. For her full moment had been gathered by the Metaphysical poets into a world of philosophy, of science and learning and the Four Last Things. The "Let us be very strange and well-bred"[18] of Congreve's Millamant (it is prose, but Congreve was a poet too, and the borrowed phrase may be allowed) rises in poetry to the "By our first strange

16 The rest of this paragraph considers poets who made use of the name Celia or who Williams considers also contained the actual and the potential as he sets out. They are listed in detail in the End note.

17 Let us descend now therefore from this top
Of speculation
Milton, *Paradise Lost*, XII. 588–9.

18 Let us be very strange and well-bred: let us be as strange as if we had been married a great while; and as well-bred as if we were not married at all.

Congreve, *The Way of the World*, IV. 1
(the proviso scene).

and fatal interview" of Donne,[19] and (though later in time) to the "Strange fits of passion" of Wordsworth.[20] Fate enters into the movement, and hostile gods; Marvell's appeal to his Coy Mistress is mightier in its demurrer than in its invitation. But it is in the *Anatomy of the World*[21] that the ascension into great poetry is most greatly exposed, and of love into more than love. Celia—or to be accurate, Elizabeth Drury—died. "Shee, shee is dead; shee's dead." Death which takes away the femininity enlarges the poetry; her death is at once a positive and a negative thing, and under its influence the world changes. The immediate application of the lesser poetry found a universality of experience in its subject. That greater moment was declared in the Moneta of *Hyperion*,[22] although Moneta is, precisely as the poem declares her to be, rather a memory than an actuality. The things that Moneta remembers are fully in poets greater than Keats, less fully in others his equals, and glimpsed again in others less than he. Some sense of them is in so strange and failing a poem as Ebenezer Jones's 'Ways of Regard';[23] they are declaimed, defined, and overruled in Chapman;[24] the dying

19 Elegy XVII.

20 One of the five poems commemorating a mysterious Lucy who has died.

21 Long poem by Donne, later titled *The First Anniversarie*, commemorating the death of Elizabeth Drury, a fourteen year old girl. Donne had never met her but became friends with her parents. The poem idealizes the dead girl; Donne told Ben Jonson that 'he described the idea of a Woman and not as she was'. The quoted line is 237.

22 Moneta, from Keats's *Fall of Hyperion* (not the first *Hyperion* as Williams suggests), was a Roman goddess of warning. Williams's reference is to her speech at 241–8. She is later in the poem (331) addressed as Mnemosyne, memory. She does appear, but only under this name, in the first *Hyperion*, III. 82 ff..

23 Ebenezer Jones (1820–1860) was a Victorian poet commended by Dante Gabriel Rossetti.

24 Williams provided excerpts from several of Chapman's plays in his anthology.

agony of Faustus,[25] the living agony of Troilus,[26] the immortal agony of Satan's living death in the Niphates speech[27] and in the reply to Christ[28] contain them. The single Celian moment becomes aware of its vast scope. It is enlarged into the terrible passion of the Adam and Eve of Paradise Lost. Celia has become the Mother of all Living, and the language of her poetry is no longer the intense delight of a day but the root of life:

> thou to me
> Art all things under heaven, all places thou.
>
> Eve to Adam, *Paradise Lost*, XII. 17–8

The language of such moments is applicable to more than the persons who utter them; like the hinted solitaries whom Wordsworth fearfully met on roads or moors or in London itself, they become super-personal by the mere intensity of their personalities. They take on the knowledge of hell. In this the Metaphysicals, and Milton beyond them, went even beyond Shakespeare, for they imagined hell, and whatever may be thought of the doctrine of hell theologically and morally, it is a very great poetic idea. Shakespeare's people were able—they were compelled—altogether to die. Lear, outraging nature, was outraged by nature, but he died. Macbeth, self-robbed of sleep, found a living somnambulism, but he died. They glanced at that other vision in moments—"Hell is murky". But it is Satan whose everlasting and hopeless desire restored the full vision

---

25 The last speech of Faustus in Marlowe's play.

26 Troilus's speech on witnessing his betrayal by Cressida, which begins, 'This she? No, this is Diomed's Cressida' from Shakespeare's *Troilus and Cressida*, V. 2. 135ff.. Williams attached great importance to this speech in his interpretation of Shakespeare, in *The English Poetic Mind*, 59ff..

27 *Paradise Lost*, IV. 32–113.

28 *Paradise Regained*, III. 203–22.

to English verse, the "perishing everlastingly" of that great
Ode, the Athanasian Creed[29]

> I would be at the worst; worst is my port,
> My harbour, and my ultimate repose,
> *Paradise Regained*, III. 209–210

and he cannot be.

On the other hand Shakespeare renewed the Celian moment
with a new perfection; It became the moment of Marina
and Perdita and Imogen and Miranda;[30] it even hovered on
the verge of more than humanity when a kind of earthly-
immortality rang in Ariel after the earthly-mortality had been
closed in the Dirge over Imogen.[31] Those lines are in the *Oxford
Book*, and are not repeated here. But the speech of Prospero,[32]
familiar though it is, is given, for it too, in its own grave way,
instructed by Ariel, enters through love and pardon as gentle as
Prospero could make it, on the topmost consciousness of poetry.
The Dirge carries perhaps more than has been supposed; all of
Celia that could die died to that sound and there was left only
the music of the spheres that Pericles heard and the pure vision

29 The Athanasian Creed appears in the *Book of Common Prayer*
under the title *Quicunque vult*, its opening words in Latin, and
begins: 'Whosoever will be saved: before all things it is necessary
that he hold the Catholick Faith. | Which Faith except every
one do keep whole and undefiled: without doubt he shall perish
everlastingly.' Williams repeats his characterisation of it as a 'great
humanist Ode' and discusses it in detail in *The Descent of the Dove*,
London 1950, 58–60, first published 1939.
30 The heroines respectively of *Pericles*, *The Winter's Tale*, *Cymbeline*
and *The Tempest*.
31 This begins, 'Fear no more the heat o' th' sun | Nor the furious
winter's rages', *Cymbeline*, IV. 2. 259ff..
32 This begins, 'Ye elves of hills, brooks, standing lakes, and groves',
The Tempest, V. 1. 33 ff..

of the translucent passion of Miranda: "O brave new world!"[33]
Against that simplicity of vision even the victories of Milton are
more human.

> Sole victor, from the expulsion of his foes,
> Messias his triumphal chariot turned
> > *Paradise Lost*, VI. 801[34]

is the spirit triumphant, but

> So singular in each particular
> That all your acts are queens[35]

is the spirit reborn. If there was any poet who could show us
more—there was one, and he was Dante.

This book ends with the death of Gerard Hopkins; it is at
once an accidental and a deliberate choice. For, setting aside
the fact that the moment makes a convenient pause before
unredeemed tradition plunged into one of its recurrently
ghastly pits, and redeemed tradition underwent one of its
periodical phoenix-changes, there is another justice in the
conclusion. It is the moment of the close of the myths. English
verse had carried in its tradition a continual use of the myths—
of Achilles, Alexander, Arthur, of the fables and the religions,
especially of that greatest of the myths (whatever energy of
morals or statement of fact it justly carries, it must necessarily
be a myth in poetry), Christianity. In the Nineties there were

---

33 *The Tempest*, V. i. 183.
34 Christ on defeating the rebel angels in the war in heaven.
35 Florizel to Perdita:
> Each your doing,
> So singular in each particular,
> Crowns what you are doing in the present deeds,
> That all your acts are queens.
> > *The Winter's Tale*, IV. 4. 143–6.

two poets of importance, Mr. Kipling and Mr. Yeats; one tended to turn from the myths, the other to translate them into his own parables. Social and philosophical changes accentuated a change in the imagination. Where Tennyson and even Hardy had occasionally been a little sad about their loss of simple faith, the newer poets much more healthily forgot it. The wistful atheist disappeared. Christianity became to every poet either a necessity or a nuisance, and the lesser myths in general became more and more merely a nuisance. Flecker and Francis Thompson picturesquely delayed them a little; Mr. Eliot for a moment recovered Agamemnon; Mr. Chesterton made them ceremonial with apocalypse. But in general, in public, they were done, and it was time. Hector and Solomon, Helios and Odin, had had a long day, and it may be that still some poet may find them necessary; if so, it will be private compulsion rather than public habit. Pan is dead.

Yet the real change was deeper than the mere disuse of myth; it was in the new use, not merely of myth but of metaphor and all knowledge. Of old these things were, no doubt, what all poetry must be, an expression of the creating mind. The divine Apollo, and even Milton's divine Messias, necessarily looked like men. They had however been removed as far as possible into divinity and heaven; they were meant as gods. Now they, if they are ever used, they and all that is used, even the divinities of machinery and the Republic, are realised as states of awareness. The most important things now in our self consciousness are the conscious knowledge of our consciousness and our revolt against our knowledge. It is this which gives rise to our significant diagrams and our private poems; the consummation of the Romantic habit. We have fulfilled the Romantics in escaping from them. There has, it is true, been renewed also a deliberate objectivity, as there have been renewed deliberate morals. A new vision of an extreme subjectivity with a freer objectivity is, it seems, approaching. If so, we may recover drama which we have largely lost since Pope wrote the close of the *Dunciad.* He did not write plays—no, but he was our last intensely dramatic poet. It is to him and Milton that we return.

All this has happened since Gerard Hopkins died, and Gerard Hopkins was the last notable poet of the myths—with two or three rare exceptions among the living. At that turn therefore this collection stops; a provisional new map of known stars amidst our study of what others now

Emerge and shine upon the Aral Sea.
Matthew Arnold, *Sohrab and Rustum*, last line

End note: detailed references for note 16

Ben Jonson's lyric 'Come my Celia, let us prove | While we may, the sports of love' appeared first in his play *Volpone* (1607) and then in his collection *The Forest* (1616); it is one of his best-known lyrics.

The forgotten poet William Percy published his *Sonnets to Coelia* in 1594; C. S. Lewis considered them 'worthless'.

As You Like It is the only Shakespeare play with a character actually named Celia but Williams seems to be thinking of the women of the comedies more generally.

Neaera was a figure from Roman love poetry, referred to by Milton, who was educated at Cambridge:
    Were it not better done as others use,
    To sport with Amaryllis in the shade,
    Or with the tangles of Neaera's hair.
        Lycidas, 67–9.

Jonathan Swift's 'The Progress of Beauty' and 'The Lady's Dressing Room' both portray a character named Celia, satirising

The Celian Moment

bodily functions and makeup. The climactic line of the latter poem is 'Oh! Celia, Celia, Celia shits!'

Alexander Pope's epigram 'Celia', now considered of doubtful authenticity, begins:
Celia, we know, is sixty five
Yet Celia's face is seventeen.

The 'illumination of Shelley' refers to the idealized Teresa (Emilia) Viviani of his poem *Epipsychidion*. See Introduction.

Christabel is an unfinished poem by Coleridge.

The Abyssinian maid is in 'Kubla Khan':
A damsel with a dulcimer
In a vision once I saw:
It was an Abyssinian maid.
'Kubla Khan', 37–9.

3

The Story of the *Aeneid*

I

Publius Virgilius Maro was born on 15 October 70 B.C., near Mantua in North Italy. His father was a farmer and a Roman citizen. He went to school at Milan, then a kind of university town, and at eighteen went on to Rome, where he belonged to a group of young men, greatly concerned with poetry and its possible new developments. With this group, such a group as always exists in any great centre of government and civilization, he studied and read for some ten years, making friends who were afterwards to be useful to him in his career.

The Roman state had been passing, from a time preceding Virgil's birth, through a series of violent crises, involving military dictatorships, civil wars, massacres, and banishments. These had at last resolved themselves into a conflict between the supporters of the old aristocratic republican government and Julius Caesar, fresh from his victories in and settlement of Gaul, supported by his army and by very widespread popular feeling. He eventually defeated Pompey, the general of the aristocratic army, overcame his supporters in Spain and

Africa, and returned to Rome, where he was in effect voted into supreme control of all branches of the administration. But before he had been able to carry out his schemes for the pacification of the Roman world, he was assassinated (44 B.C.) by a small group of republican senators. The assassination, and the campaign that followed, failed, however, to restore the older form of government. The Caesarians, led by Octavian (Caesar's nephew), Mark Antony (Caesar's Master of the Horse), and Lepidus who were called the 'triumvirs' finally defeated the enemy at Philippi in Greece. Octavian returned to Rome and Antony took over the government of the East.

During the settlement of Octavian's soldiers on the land in Italy, Virgil's property was confiscated by the Government. His father was dead, but by now some of his friends were occupying important posts in the administration, and through their good offices Virgil was compensated for the loss. He was also brought to the notice of Octavian and his minister Maecenas. The Octavian circle was rapidly becoming something like a court, by which the arts were encouraged and to which their practitioners thronged. In 37 B.C. Virgil published his first book, the *Eclogues*, which brought him at once a great reputation. He followed this, seven years after, by the *Georgics*, undertaken at the suggestion of Maecenas.

Meanwhile war had broken out between Octavian and Antony, supported by Cleopatra, Queen of Egypt. In 31 B.C. the Eastern fleets were defeated by Octavian in a sea-battle at Actium on the coast of Greece, and in the next year both Antony and Cleopatra committed suicide in Alexandria, thus leaving Octavian in undisputed control of the whole Roman world. He returned to Rome, where he was saluted as the saviour of the whole state, and received the title Augustus. He ruled until his death in A.D. 14, and his genius settled and directed the peace, civilization and dominion of Rome.

It was with the glory of this idea of Rome that Virgil now determined to fill the great epic poem which he had been preparing to write. The actual writing occupied the rest of his life. In 25 B.C. Augustus wrote from Spain to ask for news of his progress; in 23 B.C. he is said to have listened to Virgil reading three Books aloud; in 19 B.C. Virgil thought that another three years would see it finished. But in that very summer he started on a tour of the coast of Greece and was compelled by ill-health to return. He died at Brindisi in South Italy on 21 September, 19 B.C.

His personal appearance is only known from one mosaic, discovered in 1896. 'It is not only in itself well executed, but is clearly copied from a very fine picture, painted at a time when authentic portraits of Virgil were numerous, and when a live tradition of his appearance may have still survived. This portrait shows him such as he is described in his ancient biographies, and such as we can well believe him to have really been in his latter years. The face is thin and worn, the complexion sallow; the delicate features bear traces of habitually poor health. The hair is dark brown, showing flecks of grey; the forehead finely moulded; the mouth sensitively delicate; the eyes large, deeply set, and luminous'.[1]

II

'It may be safely asserted', says Professor George Gordon, 'that no single poet has exercised over the poetic production of this country so long and so continuous a control as Virgil. From Aldhelm to Bridges is the bluntest statement of its range'.[2] He goes on to name some of the writers who have received that

1   J. W. Mackail, Introduction to [his edition of] the *Aeneid*, Oxford 1930. [CW]
2   *Virgil in English Poetry*, George Gordon, Milford [i.e. Oxford University Press], 1933. [CW]

control. Bede, Chaucer, Marlowe, Spenser, Milton, Dryden (by whose translation it came about that 'Virgil entered the eighteenth century an English citizen'), Thomson, Burke, Wordsworth, Keats, Shelley, Coleridge, Landor, Arnold, Tennyson. It is impossible here to enter into the complexity of that control, of the multitudinous influences which Virgil shed over English poetry. But it may be permitted to name a few.

(I) He was, of course, at the beginning the historical bridge between the first and second Rome, between the classic writers and the medieval writers. In the myths of the Middle Ages he was turned into a magician; he became Duke Virgil of Mantua; he was fabled to have built a tower that stood on one claw, and to have done many other marvellous feats. One of his poems—the Fourth Eclogue—was supposed to have been written as an inspired prophecy of the birth of Christ. But even without such wonders, his fame was sufficient. It was by no accident of personal love alone that the greatest of medieval poets, Dante, took Virgil as his master, and imagined himself as led by Virgil upon his journey through Hell and Purgatory. For Virgil was the great poet of human life, and of civilized human life,[3] culminating in that Roman Empire which the Middle Ages supposed themselves to have revived and sanctified as the 'Holy Roman Empire'. The Middle Ages, like the period in which Virgil himself lived, regarded the institution of the Roman Empire, whether his or theirs, as being of the first importance, and as meant to command the obedience of all men. Virgil had seen and sung its foundation: their own poetry answered and reflected his.

(II) He was one of the greatest of romantic poets. Three sides of this may be briefly mentioned. (i) There was, first of all, his

3 See Section III. [CW]

feeling for Nature; a feeling exact in its details, and yet laden with a content which is certainly not Wordsworthian, but from which Wordsworth might have learned. His river-gods (cf. Tiber[4]) and his sea-nymphs[5] are neither rivers nor waves, and yet they are not merely gods inhabiting those places. A kind of strange life, inhuman, and yet aware of humanity, moves in them. Juturna in the Twelfth Book is a river-goddess and the sister of Turnus at once, and it is precisely in the agonizing union of those two facts that her fate lies. But in general man is not so closely allied to the natural powers. Only all through Virgil, Nature, though he knows as much about her as the most practical farmer, enters with a strangeness, and the moons that shine upon his forest-walks or sea-shores illumine landscapes which all Europe has borrowed for a thousand years. Professor Gordon indicates one of the most famous borrowings:

> In such a night
> Stood Dido with a willow in her hand
> Upon the wild sea-banks, and waft her love
> To come again to Carthage.
> > Shakespeare, *Merchant of Venice*, V. 1. 9.

Virgil never said *that* about Dido; but it is the kind of thing that Shakespeare could never have said had not Virgil been capable of saying similar things first.

(ii) There was, secondly, that favourite theme of romantic poets, unhappy love. The next section must discuss the relation of this to the whole *Aeneid*. Here it is enough to point out how completely and triumphantly Virgil created the deserted lover, and what intensity of feeling he gave her. 'The Roman poetry of the loyal heroine taught Europe the eloquence of love.'[6] He

---

4 *Aeneid*, VIII. 31ff..
5 *Aeneid*, X. 219–248.
6 Gordon, *Virgil in English poetry*, 43, paraphrasing W. P. Ker:

taught Europe to weep over Dido; her pyre has burned down the centuries.[7]

(iii) There is, lastly, what Matthew Arnold calls the Virgilian cry,

> The sense of tears in mortal things.
>
> *Geist's Grave*, 15–6, quoting *Aeneid*, I. 462

The 'exquisite pathos',[8] the real sadness and the sense of sadness, 'the pity of it',[9] is largely Virgil's. The hopeless hope of the souls who 'stretch out their hands towards the other bank'[10] is precisely Virgil. He drew into the light of poetry, of a poetry as intense as it was tender, and as psychologically accurate as it was poetically proportioned, the half-lights and the dusk of experience—in thought and feeling. The fall of Palinurus from the ship and Aeneas steering[11] is indescribably moving. Lavinia never speaks a word all through the poem; once she blushes,[12] and in that blush she stands rosed for ever and individualized for ever. All this is in Virgil something too great to be called 'sensibility', but it is a profound sensitiveness alive to every delicate degree of what is felt and of what is felt to be felt. He knew the very beating of the blood when it hardly dares know itself.

'But what made by far the strongest impression on the Middle Ages was . . . the poetry of the loyalty of the heroines, the fourth book of the *Aeneid*, the *Heroides* of Ovid and certain parts of the *Metamorphoses*', *Epic and Romance*, London 1908, 346.

7   *Aeneid*, IV. 646ff..

8   The phrase is from a review of Arnold's poetry by Leslie Stephen, *Saturday Review*, September 1867.

9   *Othello*, IV. I. 191.

10 *Aeneid*, VI. 314.

11 *Aeneid*, V. 855ff..

12 *Aeneid*, XII. 64–6.

So much for Virgil the medieval and Virgil the romantic. Virgil the great author of the *Aeneid* had better have his own section.

III

The subject of the *Aeneid* is single—it is the Founding of Rome. There is, however, a second subject, which, though subordinate in the poem, is in fact the cause of the poem, and therefore its true subject; and that is the salvation and settlement of Rome by Caesar Augustus. The two subjects are interwoven, and their relation is best shown in the description of the shield which Vulcan made for Aeneas; there, in the centre, was figured the decisive victory of Augustus over Antony and Cleopatra at the naval battle of Actium. In Shakespeare's *Antony and Cleopatra* Caesar is made to say that, if he conquers,

> the three-nook'd world
> Shall bear the olive freely.
> *Antony and Cleopatra*, IV. 6. 6.

This idea of peace and restoration which is only one element in the Shakespearean play is the full theme of the *Aeneid*. We do Shakespeare less than justice habitually by underrating the passion which Caesar, in the play, possesses; he is no improper antagonist for Antony just because he represents the whole civic and universal idea of unity and peace. But Shakespeare did not choose to put that idea forward as Virgil puts it forward. To Virgil, Augustus was almost a divine saviour, if not quite. The world had peace; the civil wars of a century were concluded, and the order and genius of Rome were free to impose themselves on an otherwise chaotic world.

The genius of Rome, however, was represented to him by the genius of Augustus, and he turned that in his poem to a representation of the genius of Aeneas. The great characteristic of Aeneas is his 'piety'; others—Hector, for example, as

Diomedes explains in Book XI[13]—equal him in courage, but in piety he is pre-eminent. Now piety in this sense means a very great deal. It is the honourable fulfilment of all moral duties—duties to the gods, duties to his country, duties to his family, duties to his friends. Aeneas is a man rooted in the decencies of religion and of civilization. The history of Europe since Virgil wrote has made it a little difficult sometimes for those of the West to understand the full Virgilian passion. We lose interest, for example, in the continual sacrifices; we are not moved by the perpetual reverence of Aeneas for his father Anchises on which Virgil so strongly insists; and above all we are apt completely to misunderstand his attitude towards the relation of Dido and Aeneas. For we tend to think of Aeneas as betraying Dido by sailing away from Carthage, but Virgil thought of him as betraying Rome—or coming near it—by stopping in Carthage at all, once the storm had stopped. It is Rome which is important, not Aeneas's feelings or Dido's or in fact anyone's; there was never a poet with less care for the individual than Virgil. It is true he has also an intense care for the individual; the death of Dido, like the death of Pallas later, is an agonizing business, and Aeneas feels it so. But he has no doubt what he ought to do—what in fact he *must* do: morality in this sense is one with that Necessity which is another name for Destiny or his Fate. This Necessity is something that lies behind Omnipotent Jove himself; it might be said that Jove's omnipotence consists largely in his knowing what Necessity means, and in utterly fulfilling it. The other gods struggle against it, or seek to postpone it, or appeal to Jove against it, though they never have any real hope of altering it. But Jove never expends his everlasting deity on such futile efforts.

And as Jove above, so Aeneas below. His destiny is to found Rome. Whether, in fact, he could utterly reject this is perhaps a point for discussion. It is clear he has some kind of choice

13 *Aeneid*, XI. 291–2.

in his actions; he *could* stop with Dido. But it would mean a hopeless kind of defiance of something which will not be thwarted. Rome has to get itself founded and Aeneas has to help it, and the exact point to which the will of Aeneas assents or is compelled to this is a point for our abstract discussion perhaps, but has not much to do with the poem. For Aeneas is there the kind of man who does accept this Necessity; he is *pius*,[14] he is *bonus*,[15] he is the virtuous man. Dido, poor creature, does not in the least understand the kind of man she has got hold of, nor the object of his journey, nor the sin he realizes he is committing, nor the existence of the gods, nor anything but Aeneas's face and figure and certain of his less important characteristics. The terrible phrase she flings at him—'*guest*, since that word alone is left of our marriage'[16]—is a harrowing cry, a great poetic invention. But it is ironically right—Virgil put it there for its rightness from Aeneas's point of view as well as Dido's. That is all he is; that is all he can be. 'Guest'—yes, he should never have delayed to be more. Rome is the important thing.

Such a passionately impersonal view, united with every kind of passionate personal view, is a mark of great poets. Virgil has it; Dante has it—the *Inferno* is full of it; Milton has it; Shakespeare has it. It is absolutely necessary to any comprehension of them. They will break our hearts with the agony of this or that man and woman, but their own poetic hearts are always steeled. They go on; we want to stop, and no wonder. But it is better for us to let ourselves be made to go on.

14 *Pius* in Latin has a much wider range of meaning than *pious* in English: 'In many instances *pius* undoubtedly embraces both ideas of piety towards the gods and affection to family or friends or State', Cyril Bailey, *Religion in Virgil*, Oxford 1935, 83.

15 Good.

16 *Aeneid*, IV. 323–4.

All the future of Rome, therefore, is over the poem. Aeneas grows in stature as the poem proceeds, and he becomes more and more one with, as he comes nearer and nearer to, the founding of the City. And (remark!) it is a City, not a race, which is to be founded, an established order fit for dominion. There is again no outcry for local freedoms in Virgil, though (again) there is much recognition of local passion. The universal thing, and nothing less, is to be served. No modern empire—anyhow, no modern successful empire—has ever come anywhere near entertaining the large simplicity of Virgil's claims for and belief in Rome. Rome is to order the world; but then she is first to order herself.

IV

The *Aeneid* begins with the Fall of Troy through the stratagem of the Greeks (the cause of the Trojan war is given in *Aeneid*, I. 23–32). It recounts the ill-success of Aeneas in the night's fighting and his eventual retreat from the city to the hills, where a fleet is built and from where the voyage is begun. The order of Virgil's books has been altered here in order that the story may be followed directly and to avoid the indirectness of the account which Aeneas gave to Dido. The verse quotations are generally from Dryden's version (published in 1697). A good deal of modern critical opinion tends to regard Dryden's version as nearer to the Virgilian poetry than any other. It will be remarked especially that his manner of using personifications corresponds closely to the Virgilian Gods, Nymphs, and spiritualized equalities of man. It may perhaps be added that two great English poets dealt deliberately either with Virgil or with his subject. Virgil himself appears reading his *Aeneid* aloud in Ben Jonson's *Poetaster*, 1601; and no smaller poet than Marlowe worked on the Carthaginian episode in his *Tragedie of Dido*, 1594.

4

Religion and Love in Dante: The Theology of Romantic Love

The title of this paper is not intended to propagate Christianity by arousing a factitious sense of the excitements of Theology. The assurance that Christianity is or ought to be thrilling, whether as an adventure or a catastrophe, is in danger perhaps of being a little overdone. Christianity, like all religions, is, frequently, almost unmitigated boredom or even a slow misery, in which the command to rejoice always is the most difficult of all.

The word 'romantic' is used here in some such defining sense as the words Pastoral, Moral, Dogmatic, or Mystical; it means theology as applied to a particular state—that of romantic love. I am not pretending that this is a theological treatise; it is no more than an opening of the possibility. It is convenient to begin that opening by considering the work of a great poet because the accuracy of poets presents us with definite statements, and convenient to begin with Dante because Dante is generally accepted as a great Christian poet, and there will be few doubts as to his orthodoxy. Also because he did the thing better than anyone else. The Dacre Press has already published one paper on Dante, treating his thought in special relation to the present time.[1] The present paper proposes only to discuss it in relation to that human experience of 'falling-in-love', from which Dante's own imagination began to work and the process and final possibilities of which he explored.

Two points must first be raised. The first is that this, it will be said, has often been done before. That, to an extent, is true. But it may be answered (i) that it can hardly be done too often, (ii) that we do not hitherto seem to have learnt much by what has been done. We seem to be able to denounce divorce much more easily than we can explain marriage. It is true the Dantean way is not confined to marriage, otherwise its principles could not apply to any known love—in marriage, in the family, in friendship, which they probably do. But it is also true that marriage is a unique opportunity of following that way. Marriage becomes a Way of the Soul. It is the elucidation of that kind of Way of the Soul with which Dante was concerned.

The second point is the use of the word 'Imagination'. It is generally employed to mean a vague and uncontrolled fancy. In fact, it needs only right direction, and it may then become power. Wordsworth said it was 'absolute power'.[2] It may become the union of the mind and the heart with a particular vision.

---

1   [Lucy Redpath] *Dante and the Present War*, 1941. [CW] The Dacre Press was also the publisher of this essay of Williams as a pamphlet.

2   This spiritual Love acts not nor can exist
    Without Imagination, which, in truth,
    Is but another name for absolute power
    And clearest insight, amplitude of mind,
    And Reason in her most exalted mood.
                    The Prelude (1850 text), XIV. 188–192.

Certain of the poets, by their own particular visions, have
supplied us with a pattern of life. This, certainly, is only part
of their special energy, and whether their pattern is useful to
us or not has nothing to do with our judgement or enjoyment
of them as poets. But to understand their patterns has. It is
afterwards for us to decide whether one or other pattern is a
pattern on which we choose to meditate. We shall, therefore,
be concerned here not so much with the consideration of
Dante as a poet, as with that pattern of life which is a part of
his poetry, and which he made evident to us by means of his
poetry. It need not, of course, be applicable to our own lives in
every detail, but the general principle may be. It is realistic or it
is nothing; it is accurate or it is nothing. If it is regarded merely
as a beautiful poetic dream, the dynamics of it will be lost. 'The
poet and the dreamer are distinct.'[3]

Dante's work, for our present purpose, is divisible into three
groups, (i) the *New Life*, (ii) the *Banquet*, the *On Monarchy*,
and other prose works, (iii) the *Comedy*, which is in three parts,
(a) *Hell*, (b) *Purgatory*, (c) *Paradise*. I use the English names for
convenience.[4] The *Comedy* is usually called the *Divine Comedy*,
but Dante himself gave it the shorter name; the adjective
was added later. The beginning of the whole vision is at the
beginning of the first book, the *New Life*. It is concerned
with what, in our modern language, is called 'Boy meeting
Girl'. At the age of nine Dante met at a party another child,
almost nine, by whose appearance he was thrilled; he met her
again and again, and at the age of eighteen he realized that
he was deeply in love. That is the simple statement; a young
man met a young woman, somewhere about the year 1283,

---

3 Keats, *The Fall of Hyperion*, 199.

4 The original titles are *La Vita Nuova* or *Nova*, *Il Convivio*,
   Monarchia (in Latin), the *Commedia* consisting of *Inferno*,
   Purgatorio and *Paradiso*. Williams also mentions later *On the
   Common Speech*, whose original Latin title is *de Vulgari Eloquentia*.

in the streets of Florence, and he fell in love. She, so far as we know, did not. That, however, was an accident of their personal lives. What follows, speaking generally, is to the very end of his work an account of what Dante thought, said, and did about this remarkable state of affairs. Had Beatrice, which was either her name or the name he gave her, fallen in love with him, the Way that he followed might have been less or more difficult; it would perhaps have been different in certain respects, but it could hardly have been very different in its essential nature.

He was then, in the most literal sense, 'shocked' by this experience, and (as poets will) he made immediate attempts to understand and define it to himself. It may be said here at once that the whole possibility of Dante's vision being useful to us depends on what view we take of 'falling in love'. Dante, except that he was a great poet, was apparently a normal young man—selfish, proud, hot-tempered, sexually alert, busy with a lot of affairs, especially with politics. He was born in 1265; he did his military service at 24; he was, as one might say, Mayor of the City at 35; he was an omnivorous reader, interested in art and science and theology. There was, except for that capacity of ordering his vision in great poetry, nothing unusual about him. But it is, of course, open to us to deny that most young people fall in love as Dante did, and that they see a particular person of the opposite sex in a blaze of beauty and goodness. It may be that all that is only a literary tradition. I do not myself think it is; I think it is a normal human emotion. It may or may not be accompanied, or very quickly followed, by the direct sexual emotion; generally it is. In Dante's case it certainly was; we know this because he says so. He discovered that the sight of Beatrice produced three reactions in him. He attributed them (as was the habit of the physiological science of his day, and therefore also a literary habit) to three centres of the human body—the heart, the brain, and the liver. The heart, where (to him) 'the spirit of life' dwelled, exclaimed to him, at that first meeting: 'Behold a god stronger than I, who is to come and rule over me'. The brain declared: 'Now your beatitude has appeared to you'. And the liver (where natural emotions, such as sex, inhabited) said 'O misery! how I shall be disturbed henceforward!'[5]

He is, it seems, 'satisfied' by Beatrice; his sensations, his emotions, his ideas, his faith, coalesce. Perfection in some strange sense exists, and walks down the street of Florence to meet him. She is 'the youngest of the Angels'; her image in his thought 'is an exultation of Love to subdue him', yet so perfect that Love never acts without 'the faithful counsel of reason, wherever such counsel was useful to be heard';[6] she is 'the destroyer of all evil and the queen of all good';[7] she is the equivalent of heaven itself. I will repeat again that it is for Dante's readers to determine whether they think this to be a normal state for a young man in love or not. I do not say universal; I will not claim that it is true of everyone. But if it is true of a very large number, as it seems on the evidence to be, then we had better determine what kind of attention we are going to give it. If it is this which often leads to marriage, then we shall not understand marriage unless we understand this; if it is this which sometimes breaks up marriage, then still more we ought to understand it. If, as in Dante's own personal case, it neither leads to marriage nor breaks up marriage, then it may still be one of the more important human experiences, as it was to Dante.

The *New Life* continues to give an account of this relationship. It was, objectively, a very slender relationship. Beatrice and Dante were certainly on speaking terms, but that is about all we know. We know that because at one time she had heard

---

5   *Vita Nuova*, II.
6   *Ibid.* Williams here but not invariably uses the translation by Dante Gabriel Rossetti.
7   *Vita Nuova*, X.

tales about him and she cut him dead in the street,[8] It is this incident which provides him with an opportunity to describe what meeting her meant to him—what meeting the boy or girl has (it is our present thesis) meant to thousands of similar girls or boys. He says that when she met him in the street and said good-morning, he was so highly moved that he was, for the moment, in a state of complete goodwill, complete *caritas*[9] towards everyone. If anyone had at that moment done him an injury, he would necessarily have forgiven him. He has not only fallen in love; he is, strictly, 'in love'. He is aware of that beyond everything; 'if anyone had asked me a question I should have been able to answer only "Love".'[10] This would sound sentimental were it not for Dante's careful use of other words. It is a 'Love' which necessarily forgives injuries; or rather, it does so because it is indeed Love. And therefore he calls her salutation 'blessed', because it is beatitude which it inspires. In fact, he becomes for one moment in his soul that Perfection which he has observed in Beatrice.

I repeat that Dante was no sentimentalist. He knew that in that fortunate state he experienced, according to its degree, beatitude. But he does not suggest that that state is fixed in him. He adored the Glory in Beatrice, as thousands of us have; he became the Glory in himself by a simple communication

---

8 I am aware of the literary convention of Dante's time, a convention adequately and effectively discussed in Mr. C. S. Lewis's *Allegory of Love*. But a literary convention is, at its best, a means of passion. [CW] The incident is in *Vita Nuova*, X.

9 Dante's Italian is *caritade*; *caritas* is the Latin equivalent; both translate Greek *agape* (see note 11 below). 'The definition of the kingdom . . . is the establishment of a state of *caritas*, or pure love, the mode of expansion of one moment into eternity', Williams, *He Came Down from Heaven*, Chapter V.

10 *Vita Nuova*, XI.

of grace. Love, charity, *agape*,[11] was for the moment inevitable. But it was to be a long time before he could himself become that state permanently. It was indeed, as we can see from a consideration of all his work, his whole problem: could he indeed become the Glory which he saw and by which for a moment he had been transfused? It was his problem as it has been and remains the life-problem of many others. The rest of Dante's work is a pattern of the Way. 'I have been', he said soon after that description, 'at that point of life beyond which he who passes cannot return';[12] and this indeed is the description of such a 'falling in love'—it is a region from which no creature returns afterwards. One is never the same again.

The *New Life* has in it many very pleasant and agreeable lesser incidents not unlike those of any young man in love. He wrote verse about her (but it happened to be good verse); he tried to avoid being publicly supposed to be attracted by her. But the next passage to which there is room here to draw attention is a kind of curious meditation—possibly of very high significance, possibly not; the reader must judge. He sees one day a girl coming towards him (all Dante's devotion to Beatrice did not prevent him noticing such other incidents) whose name was Joan. She was also called by her friends Primavera, or Spring. Behind her, at a little distance, was Beatrice; and Dante was struck by the thought that Joan was going before Beatrice as John the Precursor went before our Lord.[13] Unless this is serious, it is almost profane. If it is serious, it is the beginning of a very high mystical identity. Beatrice is not our Lord. But

---

11 *Agape*: the normal word in New Testament Greek for love, referring particularly to the love of God for human beings and, to the extent that we are capable, of human beings for God. In the King James Bible it is also sometimes, as in 1 Corinthians 13, translated as *charity*. See discussion in the Introduction.

12 *Vita Nuova*, XIV.

13 *Vita Nuova*, XXIV.

Beatrice has been throughout precisely the vehicle of Love, of sexual love and of the vision in sexual love. She has awakened in Dante a celestial reverie; she has appeared to him the very carriage of beauty and goodness; she has, unknowingly, communicated to him an experience of *caritas*. These are the properties of Almighty Love. What Dante is now doing is to identify the power which reposed in Beatrice with the nature of our Lord. Love had been (as he himself said) a quality; now, hardly defining it, he is on the point of seeing it as precisely the Person of Love. In that moment he justified all future lovers in a similar moment.

It is impossible, or at least undesirable, to follow this spiritual identification further here; such a study would have to be separate. We must return to the more exact intellectual meaning of the incidents, and pass on at once to the Death of Beatrice. Dante heard of it when, having left Florence on business, he was engaged in composing a poem, and he breaks off with a phrase from the *Lamentations* of Jeremiah: 'How doth the city sit solitary that was full of people! how is she become as a widow that was great among the nations!'[14]

There is no reason to suppose that the Death of Beatrice was, in Dante's own life, anything else than the death of Beatrice. She died young—she, the single girl who was the high and unmeriting cause of so much, whose single face justified, by the art of her lover, so many other faces. The women who have seriously affected great art have been few, and fewer those who have affected great theology in great art—happy if (as probably Beatrice did not) they knew of what they were the cause, happier if they took an active part in the result. She died, and even her death became vastly significant. For that sudden young death stands to us not only as an actual death of an actual girl, the princely gaiety that smiled at Dante in

14 *Vita Nuova*, XXX. quoting *Lamentations*, I.I.

Florence, but also as a vanishing of Perfection. It has been, through all time, part of the monotonous admonition of the old to the young that such rapt visions do not last, and far too often the discouraged old have implied that the mere fact of the quick passage of the vision means that it was in some sense unreliable, untrustworthy, valueless. It is false; no second experience can, of itself, destroy the value of a first experience. Yet aged imbecility has this much to be said for it—the particular Glory of the first 'falling-in-love', the living sense of Perfection, does seem to be withdrawn. Time and habit veil it perhaps. But I would rather choose to believe that it is not merely so, but that the Glory which attended the vehicle of Love operates at the will of Love. Dante has to become the thing he has seen. He has to become, by his own will, the *caritas* which was, by God's will, awakened in him at the smile of Beatrice; he has to be faithful to that great communication in the days when Beatrice does not smile. Or, if she had lived and smiled, then when she had seemed to exhibit only natural joy and not supernatural power. 'There hath passed away', wrote Wordsworth of another revelation, 'a Glory from the earth'.[15] Religion itself knows such withdrawals; 'the dark night' is asserted to be an inevitable stage of the Way. Dante knew the death of Beatrice, and many other young lovers have known the disappearance of the peculiar Beatrician quality. This is the meaning of the death in the whole pattern. It is not, however, an unfortunate accident which is a conclusion. It is a state of being, a quenching of sensitive knowledge, which is a necessary—or all but necessary—part of the Way of Romantic Love.

Beatrice, then, dies; and for the present purpose the book of the *New Life* must be left at that point.[16] The second group

15 *Immortality Ode*, 18.
16 I deliberately do not here discuss the problems of the other lady—the Lady at the Window, as she is called, because in so

of Dante's writings need not detain us long. The *Banquet* is a philosophical discussion; the *On Monarchy* a political, and the *On the Common Speech* a literary. They represent Dante's concern with general life, with, as one may say, the City of Man, especially *On Monarchy*. The principles of this have been already discussed in the other Dacre Paper (*Dante and the Present War*), and all that need be said here is that they are a necessary part of the Beatrician way. Politics are, or should be, a part of *caritas*; they are the matter to which the form of *caritas* must be applied. The *On Monarchy* is Dante exercising his capacities, the capacities illuminated by the *New Life*, but not so much concerned with Beatrice directly as with the whole effort of human relationships. They too failed in fact, as far as Dante's own life was concerned; he was exiled, condemned to death, and disreputed in Florence. This was perhaps an even greater contradiction of his vision than the death of Beatrice; with Beatrice the visible Good had disappeared, but in Florence the possible Good had been betrayed.

These two facts, which were true of his external life, seem to have been true also of his interior. Beatrice had been taken away from his sight and he had also in some sense lost fidelity to her.

short a space I wish to keep to the main path of the Way. If she were actual (as I suppose), she was in some sense a re-expression of the Glory. But then certainly it cannot have been she on whose account Beatrice rebukes Dante in the *Purgatory*. The attributions to her in the *Banquet* are more intellectual than those in the *New Life*, and she is more closely identified with Philosophy. But that is what we should expect from Dante's developing mind; she is more closely identified with Philosophy because she is, in fact, more apt to be analysed philosophically. [CW] The Lady at the Window or *donna gentile*, an allegorical personification of philosophy but also possibly an actual woman, is introduced in *Vita Nuova*, XXXV and developed in the *Convivio* books II and III. Beatrice's rebuke is in *Purgatorio*, XXX. 103–145. Williams discusses the Lady at the Window in detail in *The Figure of Beatrice*, 47–51.

The exact nature of this loss of fidelity can be conveniently discussed later. It was at this time, in exile and conscious of his own sin, but conscious no less of his own poetic genius and of what he believed to be his duty, that he set to work on the *Comedy*.

The opening of the first part of the *Comedy*, of the *Hell*, is a great and complex account of this situation. Dante 'refinds' himself; he becomes again conscious of himself. It is the morning of Good Friday, of the Betrayal and the Passion. He is middle-aged; he is lost in a dark wood; he is on a path 'more bitter than death'. Everything has gone wrong, and he has gone wrong. He sees before him a great mountain which he obscurely identifies with a desired happiness—'the occasion and beginning of our Joy'. It is not, then, further defined; a kind of nightmare is on him, and one does not define further the vivid apparitions of nightmare. He tries to reach it; all will then be well; but he cannot; three wild beasts appear on the slopes and drive him back again into the wild wood. These beasts, as in nightmare (and also in poetry), are several things at the same time. They are beasts; they are also certain evils—Lechery, Pride, Avarice; they are also the three chief periods of human life displayed by those evils. The Panther is gay and beautiful and speedy; the Lion is strong and fierce; the She-Wolf, terrible beyond the others, is fierce with an insatiable hunger. Youth and Middle Age and Old Age—and of all these Old Age, lean and insatiably greedy, is the worst. It is she who prevents the ascent and destroys what has been. Beyond is the unattainable skiey mountain, something more than temporal; behind is the dark wood of his lost misery, and to that darkness he is inevitably returning.[17]

What interferes? The love of Beatrice. The *New Life* had been about the love of Dante for Beatrice, but the *Comedy* is about

17   This paragraph and three following consider *Inferno*, I.

the love of Beatrice for Dante. She is made aware of his peril by the intervention, through St. Lucy, of the Mother of God; and she immediately acts. All that follows depends on her. This is worth noting because it is a preparation for what does follow much later in the poem. Beatrice's love of her lover may be of a more advanced kind than his for her, but it is no less passionate. When she rebukes him it is he whom she rebukes; when, in the *Paradise*, she delivers what seem rather like lectures on the movement of the stars and all that sort of thing, it is only because he very much wants to know and she happens to know; it is for his pleasure rather than hers. She teases him, she scolds him, she calls him by names of love; and in the very end it is he only at whom her eyes gaze before they plunge into the mystery of God himself. She is a divine thing, but she is also, still and always, the Florentine girl.

She moves then to her lover's rescue. But he does not at the moment know that. Great and marvellous though his experience of her had been in that 'falling-in-love', it had not been his only experience, and Dante was far too intelligent to pretend that it had. What appears to him in that nightmare, and seems for the first moment to add to the nightmare, is a kind of ghostly figure who may be anything, and whose voice, when it first speaks aloud in that disastrous forest, is hoarse from long disuse. Spectral and awful it looms, but it is Dante's only hope, in that hideous simultaneous appearance which life has put on: he appeals to it. It answers; it promises help, and presently—O dispersal of the horrid dream!—it names Mantua, Virgil's city. It is Virgil: 'My Master and my Author'—'Maestro e autore'. Now Virgil, besides being Virgil, is also everything good that is not Beatrice. 'Autore' is 'author' in Milton's sense; 'my author and disposer'. He is, particularly, poetry, the source of Dante's own style. It is clear therefore that it is very fitting that he should be sent by Beatrice—or rather not sent, for no command has been laid upon him; it is his own courtesy which has moved him. But also, since poetry is not religion, it is very fitting that he should not lead Dante into

Paradise. Virgil—poetry—may exhibit visions, and initiate conduct; it cannot be religion. This is not, of course, to say that we should, when we are writing poetry, put religion before poetry; poetry is absolute in its own place, and even Beatrice cannot command it. The voice of Virgil is his own.

The message which he brings is that the only way of safety from the she-wolf of Avarice and Age is to see 'the eternal'— the principles of the universe. These are to be shown in the three places of the dead, (i) those who desire the second death, (ii) those who are contented in the fire, (iii) the blessed. Dante accepts the vision and the way (which Beatrice has brought to him): 'Poet, by the God that poetry in itself cannot reach, lead on.'

The 'blind' world of Hell into which Dante and Virgil now enter is an ordered descent through a number of circles of sinners. This descent can be understood, as all great poetry can be, in many different ways. But one of those ways is that of the particular Beatrician vision; that is, the experience of 'falling in love' is here followed to its distant and dreadful end in a complete betrayal of itself. The first circle belongs to the great pagans who could not, as Dante saw it, be saved; it belongs, certainly, precisely to poetry and philosophy which cannot, of themselves, lead to salvation. It is where Virgil himself dwells. But after that, in the second circle of hell (but the first punishment of sin) we come to the sufferings of the incontinent, or those who have loved by their own indulgence against the moral law. With two of these Dante speaks; they are the unhappy lovers Paolo and Francesca. Now it is true that these two have sinned in their love, but it is also true that their sin is possible to all lovers, moral or immoral. It is a too great indulgence, a too long lingering in permitted delight, a lawless concentration on each other. Dante is so overcome with pity at the sight of them that he faints; and that faint is led up to by every circumstance of tenderness. What is sinful in Paolo and Francesca is, as one might say, only just sinful. Their love is beautiful, moving, faithful; what is wrong with it? Only the prolongation of the self-indulged moment. Love is lazy. But that laziness, though it is the most touching thing in hell, is yet the very opening to all hell. For what, in the very order of hell, follows?[18]

The love of Paolo and Francesca had been lovely and mutual; the next circle carries indulgence a step further. It is the circle of the gluttons, and it is clear that here gluttony has, as Dante distinctly stated that all his work had, a symbolical interpretation. Gluttony is, no doubt, gluttony, but also it is gluttony in everything, and that no longer with a companion, in a kind of sharing of even sin, but separately, but alone. The next step to preferring oneself in 'the two of us' against all else is to prefer oneself alone. And this leads, inevitably, on that lost and secret path, to hatred of others who have their own other desires; and first of all, in the vision, we are shown the soul contending against other souls, the lover of himself against the lovers of their own selves, or even the soul against itself. It is as they pass from the circle of misers and spendthrifts—the disordered desire to preserve fighting against the disordered desire to enjoy—that Virgil exclaims: 'Now let us descend into even greater misery', and they go on to the circle of mere anger. Joy has disappeared and intellect is disappearing; they enter the marsh of *accidie*, of gloom, where those who hated 'the sweet air and the sun' lie gurgling in the bubbling mud.[19]

All these are, no doubt, separate sins, but they are also in some sense a development of the same sin, the sin of indulging oneself in love instead of devoting oneself to the duty of love,

18 'Blind' is from *Inferno*, IV. 13, which canto also deals with the great pagans. Paolo and Francesca are in *Inferno*, V.

19 Gluttony is in *Inferno*, VI, the misers and spendthrifts in *Inferno*, VII. The line 'Now let us descend' is *Inferno*, VII. 97, those who hated 'the sweet air and the sun' are at VII. 122.

the perverse and selfish twisting of the 'falling-in-love' to nothing but one's own satisfaction. For every mistake made on the Way of Romantic Love there is pardon and grace; for the deliberate and continued perversion of it, there can be, by the nature of things, no pardon—'neither here nor in the world to come'.[20]

The 'greater misery' deepens. Something more like definite hate appears; the travellers are attacked; as they reach the wall of the infernal City of Dis the gates are shut against them and the devils threaten them. Something looks over the wall of the City against the sight of which Virgil covers Dante's eyes. The dark air is lit by the ever-burning mosques of hell; above them the storm whirls round the immense but narrowing funnel of the abyss; before them are the walls of iron; and below is the unknown hell of even worse horrors. When at last the poets enter the City, they are in the place of heretics. What is heresy? the clinging to a particular thought or idea because it is one's own, although it is against the known decision of the Church—the disintegrity of the intellect, the justification to oneself of error and evil. Here that self indulgence has gone very far—'and much more than you can see', says Virgil, 'the burning tombs of the heretics lie laden.'[21] Beyond are the other circles of the deliberate sinners against love by force or fraud. Eros[22] has turned wholly against itself; it is now fully that old she-wolf 'lean with insatiable cravings'. 'The pollution of all the world'[23] rises to meet them; the great torments open on

20 Not Dante but *Matthew* 12.32.

21 *Inferno*, IX. 129.

22 Eros: 'It is neither sex appetite pure and simple; nor, on the other hand, is it necessarily related to marriage. It is something like a state of adoration', Williams, *He Came Down from Heaven*, Chapter V. He illustrates it by quoting Adam in *Paradise Lost*, VIII. 546–59.

23 *Inferno*, X. 136.

every side. There is no space here to detail them. Only it may be remembered that though they are all separate, yet they are all one. It is one soul, as well as many, which is chaotic with its horrid longings; the soul which, among many interpretations, can be seen to be that which had once loved only a little in the wrong way and been content: it is more—it is the soul. or might be, as Dante very well knew, which had once seen the beauty and experienced the grace communicated by the girl's face in the streets of Florence, or any other city. There is one incident which reveals it. In one of the loathsome ditches lie a people covered by human excrement, and among them a certain woman—'a foul and dishevelled drab, scratching herself with filthy nails, and restless—now squatting, now standing'. It is Thaïs, the harlot. There had been harlots far above, in the circle of the incontinent—Cleopatra, and Helen, and others; why is Thaïs here? Because she is lost in the filth of flattery for her own gain. The frank harlots are the least of all sinners; she among the greater. One of her lovers (this is the story Dante quotes) had said to her: 'Are you very grateful to me?' and she answered: 'Beyond all measure.'[24] She had, that is, pretended in her harlotry to what is exactly true in the holy innocence of the Beatrician vision. Dante and Thaïs both said in effect 'I am infinitely grateful'. But Dante meant 'infinitely' and Thaïs did not. She scratches herself therefore for ever in the excrement of which her words were the exact image.

At the very bottom of hell everything changes. Noise ceases; fire vanishes; diseases disappear. Almost a different kind of life appears—the life of the utterly damned. Damnation itself lives, in so far as it can live; the perverse contradiction of all good. Here the damned are almost one with Hell. At the beginning the vision of the beloved had awoke Dante to courtesy and humility and goodwill; and from Beatrice he had moved to an apprehension of the mass of men, and the Divine City. Virgil

24 For Thaïs see *Inferno*, XVIII. 127–136.

and Beatrice had stood for everything, and the plain of ice
on which the poets now find themselves is the opposite of
both Virgil and Beatrice. Tears themselves are frozen within
the eyes; 'their weeping does not allow them to weep'.[25] There
the souls lie wholly covered by ice, and are indistinguishable;
no-one speaks; instead of speech there is the wind of the air
disturbed only by the monotonous beating of Satan's wings.
These are the final traitors to their 'lords and benefactors'. This
is the end of the way which had begun, so almost excusably,
with Paolo and Francesca, the spiritual treachery to which
that little indulgence must, unrepented, eventually lead; here is
Satan, 'the creature who was once so beautiful,' and is now 'the
guilty worm which pierces the world'. This, certainly, is what
love, even the love of Beatrice, or of any woman or any man
may become. 'It is time for parting: all is seen.'[26]

The poets pass from this cannibalism of the spirit to the second
great vision—the Purgatory-Paradise. Dante is to be shown
the quality of eternity. Hell is eternity without the quality
of eternity; that is, it is mere monotonous and everlasting
repetition. The new discovery is to be of repentance and re-
formation, but it is the love-planet Venus which still presides.
It begins (like Hell) with a single moment of love. Dante
meets his friend Casella, who sings to him one of Dante's own
poems, a poem which opened the third book of the *Banquet*.
The first line is: 'Love that discourses to me in my mind',[27]
and Dante insists on the 'in my mind' for it is there that this
affection for truth and virtue exists. The aspect of the beloved
'aids our faith', just as it 'renovates nature'. But the mind has
to work on it, and so has faith, and it is this which, it seems,

25 *Inferno*, XXXII. 44–8.
26 *Inferno*, XXXIV. 34, 108 and 69.
27 This canzone in praise of the Lady Philosophy, *Amor che ne la
mente mi ragiona*, is quoted by Casella at *Purgatorio*, II. 112. The
two following phrases are adapted from it, lines 53 and 29.

Paolo and Francesca have not done. There is a little delay even here. Dante and all the souls, and even Virgil, are so held by the singing that they stand listening, until the Guardian of the Place interferes—'How now, slow spirits! what delay is this? On to the Mount, strip yourselves of the slough, and let God be manifest to you',[28] and all skirr off like frightened doves.

It is Pride that is the sin purged in the first terrace of Purgatory, where moving towers of stone seem to appear, until it is found that they are sinners carrying great weights on their backs. The first intention of anyone who knows that love which Beatrice has awakened must be to rid himself of himself. The soul illuminated by that young love-vision has to make haste; it cannot itself become those virtues which were for an instant communicated to it until it attends to other than itself. But when this is done, it finds that the next purging is of Envy; without freedom from that there can be no development of love, and just as in hell the gluttony of love leads to hatred of others, so here the envious souls have their eyes sewn up, so that they cannot see others and are blind to the facts of things. 'O mortal race, why do you set your hearts to exclude partnership?'[29] This is the second demand of Purgatory that love, being humble, should be open to include; that is, that the emotion aroused by the salutation of Beatrice should become a principle of life. This is the definition of the true romantic way. It is perhaps significant that it is while Virgil is explaining that 'the more souls that love so much the more love'[30] that he promises that the sight of Beatrice in heaven will explain all. So, they are on the third terrace where a harsh smoke hides those who were guilty of Anger, and at the beginning and end of this terrace is a kind of ecstasy of gentleness, a proper introduction

28 *Purgatorio*, II. 120–3.
29 Pride is purged in Cantos X to XII, envy in Cantos XII to XIV. The quoted line is *Purgatorio*, XIV. 86–7.
30 *Purgatorio*, XV. 73–4. Anger is purged in Canto XVI.

to what happens on the fourth, Virgil's great discourse on the nature of love. Half the vision is seen; half the poem is done. It turns, as it were, on itself to move faster to its end.

Love, says Virgil in his analysis, can never turn against itself; man cannot hate himself or his Maker; whom then? his neighbour—by deliberate evil heart or by failure of love. True love may be sluggish, or it may be confused in its object, and lack proportion. 'Set love in order.'[31] 'All loves that move you arise from necessity, but power to control is in you. This noble virtue Beatrice means by free-will; have this in mind if she speaks of it.'[32] Free-will is the right control of confused love. While they are speaking the terrace is full of the purgation of sloth; many souls running with great speed. It is, in a sense, the first prospect of Paradise, and there remain but the terraces of Avarice and Gluttony and Lechery to pass, these three mounting towards heaven in that order as in hell they descend in the reverse order. It is while on this journey that Dante takes an opportunity to state the realism of his own love poetry. 'I am one', he says, 'who when love breathes in me observe it, and in the manner it dictates within go on to expound it.'[33] It was the claim of Dante to be accurate, as it was his delight. He certainly never supposed himself to be dreaming of a false spirituality, he whose initiation was accomplished by mortal eyes.

31 'Set love in order Thou that lovest me', the first line of a poem translated by Rossetti and attributed by him to St Francis of Assisi. This line in the original Italian, *Ordina quest'Amore, O tu ch' m'ami*, is on the flyleaf of the Temple Classics edition of *Purgatorio*, the edition Williams used, and is there ascribed to Jacopone da Todi, who was considered by E. G. Gardner more likely to be the author.

32 *Purgatorio*, XVIII. 70–5.

33 *Purgatorio*, XXIV. 52–4. Avarice is purged in Cantos XIX to XXI, gluttony in Cantos XXII to XXIV and lechery (lust) in Cantos XXV to XXVI.

The last terrace is a terrace of flame in which the lustful are purged, and it is when the poets have reached the end of this terrace and have to pass through a wall of fire that Virgil encourages Dante by the mention of those eyes. 'My sweet Father, to comfort me, spoke of Beatrice as he went forward, saying: "Already I seem to see her eyes".'[34] It is the last purification from an actual sin; the whole will has been healed and restored. Virgil's great line consummates the whole: 'I crown and mitre thee over thyself'.[35] The forest of the Earthly Paradise stretches before him he has, here, indeed re-found himself. It is in this renewal of himself and of earth that the Florentine girl again appears.

It is now in the Earthly Paradise, after the sins have been obliterated and the virtues re-established, that the full supernatural validity of Beatrice begins to he expressed. It had, one might suppose, been made sufficiently clear in the *New Life* and certainly if that were all that remained to us of Dante's work it would be sufficient for the religious encouragement of all lovers. But we now know that, in addition to that young enthusiasm the mature mind of Dante did not wish to establish any contrary doctrine. He takes particular care to identify the processional figure who now appears, drawn by the celestial Two-Natured Gryphon (half Lion and half Eagle) who is Christ, and accompanied by Angels, Virtues, Prophets, and Evangelists, with the very Florentine girl of the past. When he first sees her veiled figure he cries out to Virgil: 'The embers burn, Virgil, the embers burn';[36] and afterwards the Virtues of this certainly new life assure him (as if he needed it—the assurance is for us): 'These are the eyes from which Love began

34 *Purgatorio*, XXVII. 52–4.

35 *Purgatorio*, XXVII. 142.

36 *Purgatorio*, XXX. 22–48. Dante's words to Virgil are those in which Dido acknowledged to her sister Anna her feelings for Aeneas, *Aeneid*, IV. 23.

to shoot his arrows at you'.[37] And she herself, in a terrible voice, utters the same assurance in the line which has been considered the greatest in all European poetry: 'Look well; we are, we are indeed Beatrice'.[38] She is justified in it by her office, her nature, and her passion; she knows her part in him and has accepted it by her care for his salvation; she knows his duty to her and has accepted that. It is a woman who speaks; it is her last touch of mortality before the heavenly smile breaks through. She comes then, the same Beatrice, in what is called by the commentators 'the Pageant of the Church', and so it is, but it is also the pageant of Beatrice. It halts, and she speaks to him, accusing him—of what? One is not quite clear; Dante did not, in so many words, state it. It is something to do with his genius, of which she frankly reminds him; and something to do with a falsity 'to her buried flesh'.[39] But the Church itself has not insisted that a man should be faithful after her death to a woman whom he loved but had not married. Was the falsity then in some lechery? some tearing by the Panther whom he had never noosed? Or was there something more? some apostasy to the vision? If he had at some moment denied *that*, if he had apostatized from his particular Dantean vocation, if he had been not only 'wanderingly lewd'[40] but foolishly wise, and in some state of despair or other abandonment had denied the validity of Beatrice, then the bitter oration would be entirely justified. However this may be, it is to be noticed that it is still the vision in flesh which is in question. It is to 'mia carne sepulta', 'my buried *flesh*', that Beatrice demands fidelity, the flesh of the girl loved in Florence. It is infidelity to this which, when all lesser sins have been purged, demands a final purging.

37 *Purgatorio*, XXXI. 115–7.

38 *Purgatorio*, XXX. 73.

39 *Purgatorio*, XXXI. 48.

40 Paraphrase of *Purgatorio*, XXXI. 28–30.

It is after this when even this has been bathed away in Lethe that the great theological affirmation of the nature of Beatrice takes place. She gazes into the eyes of the Gryphon who is Christ, and It back into hers.[41] There it is mirrored now as one, now as the other, 'immutable in itself, mutable in its image'.[42] The Godhead and the Manhood are, as it were, deeply seen in those eyes whence Love began to shoot its arrows at Dante, by the Glory and the femininity. The moment in the *New Life* when the girl was seen as the vehicle of Love, preceded by Joan as Christ was preceded by John, is here multiplied and prolonged—one might say, infinitely. The supernatural validity of that 'falling-in-love' experience is again asserted, with every circumstance of accurate definition. In the full Earthly Paradise, she is seen mirroring the Incarnate Splendour, as in Florence its light had been about her. 'Look at him,' her attendants entreat her; 'unveil your face that he may see your second beauty.'[43] She does—and he does.

If indeed Dante had at any time denied his proper doctrine of grace, here he renewed and re-asserted it. He was now, in the poem which he had imagined her as helping to create, doing what he had wished and writing of her 'what had not heretofore been written of any woman'.[44] It has become a great classic of literature. But the question this paper is concerned to ask is not so much poetic as realistic; was Dante merely accurate? When young men and young women fall in love, is it true that they do often see each other in an unusual beauty and glory? and if so, was Dante's justification of it itself justified? I will return again to that question at the end.

It is perhaps worth while pausing here to note that, soon after this wonder of revelation, Dante permits himself a moment

41 *Purgatorio*, XXXI. 120.
42 *Purgatorio*, XXXI. 125–6.
43 *Purgatorio*, XXXI. 136–8.
44 *Vita Nuova*, ending.

of celestial laughter. He is shown a vision of the Church in apostasy, and he is moving onward with Beatrice and Matilda, who had drawn him through Lethe, when he asks a question to which he has already been told the answer. Beatrice refers him to Matilda. Matilda protests that she did really explain to him, and Beatrice with a heavenly delight answers: 'Well, yes—perhaps he *has* had other things to think of since then!'[45] She almost says, what she does say presently, 'Lamb!'

The process through Paradise begins. We are in the place of those adult in love; anyone who prefers the *Hell* may be left to the rebuke which Dante imagines Virgil addressing to him when he displayed overmuch interest in hell. 'Once more—and I shall be indignant'.[46] The general idea that the *Hell* is more interesting is true—for those who do not wish to be 'adult in love'. Dante did. The poetic problems are, no doubt, greater; it is almost a measure of Dante's genius that he overcame them as he did. He so overcame them that the reader becomes gradually aware that the interest of all the rest of his work is heightened by this; say, depends on this. Without the *Paradise*, all the rest would he great and moving; with the *Paradise*, though it remains great and moving, it yet dwindles by comparison. The first meetings with Beatrice, thrilling as they are, become less urgent in this world where 'in carità è qui *necesse*',[47] love is fate. When she speaks, here, of the 'courage'[48] of Dante's eyes, she is speaking seriously. This is the poetry of experience, and not of theory: the experience of the 'in-Godding'[49] of the self, the taking of the self into God.

45 *Purgatorio*, XXXIII. 123–5.
46 *Inferno*, XXX. 131–2.
47 *Paradiso*, III. 77: 'to be in charity is here a logical necessity'.
48 *Paradiso*, V. 3.
49 'In-Godding' renders a neologism at *Paradiso*, IV. 28.

This is the purpose and problem of the *Paradiso*: how is man in-Godded? The problem to which Beatrice is to lead him to the answer. 'From the first day when I beheld her face in this life until the present moment', Dante says, just before the full revelation of the celestial Rose, 'my song never ceased to study her'.[50] It is her eyes which his, throughout, study. But what then now are those eyes? and what is the method of the in-Godding which they behold? The whole of the *Paradise* is, as might be expected, greatly beyond our common knowledge. Not until many more lovers have set themselves to follow that Way will it become known and (as far as it ever can) common. The method is the following of the sanctity which is known and understood in romantic love and to which that love was meant to lead. The eyes of Beatrice are still to Dante the direction of the soul knowing sanctity, which is the courtesy of our Lord God, as they had already been to him the vision of the courtesy. In the first canto Dante, bidden to look at the sun, sees as it were a second sun, as if he came into a new universe which was yet the same, 'a new heaven and a new earth'.[51] The earth is certainly there; the body is there; Dante does not forget that vehicle by which all illumination of that Way came. In the fourth circle of heaven, where the great doctors and sages are, Solomon proclaims the doctrine: 'When the glorious and holy flesh shall be reclothed upon us, our persons shall be more acceptable by being more complete . . . the glow we now wear shall be less than the flesh . . . the organs of the body shall be strong to all that can give delight';[52] and all the circle, desiring their bodies, say Amen. This statement is made in answer to Beatrice inquiring on Dante's behalf. It is her business and privilege in the Paradise to supply, of herself, or from others, the instruction and knowledge he so passionately desires.

50 *Paradiso*, XXX. 28–30.
51 *Paradiso*, I. 63 to which Williams compares *Revelation* 21.1.
52 *Paradiso*, XIV. 43–60.

The flesh and the soul are one: that is the nature of the experience of beatitude. The first great maxim of beatitude is announced by the spirit of Piccarda in the first heaven: 'here love is fate'.[53] Dante has asked her whether she and those with her do not grudge the greater glory of others in more advanced Orders of heaven, and she answers, in effect, that such a question is meaningless: 'the quality of love makes quiet the will; if we desired anything other than we have, we should be a discord from his will; to be *thus* is what we most desire; his will is our peace.'[54] We love—what more? This love, each for all, has everywhere due proportion and intensity. Knowledge increases. In the heaven of Venus, beyond which the last shadow of earth does not reach, where the great lovers are, Dante sees Folco of Marseilles (a troubadour and afterwards a Cistercian), to whom he uses the great phrase: 's' io m'intuassi, come tu t'inmii', 'if I in-thee'd myself, as thou dost in-me thyself'.[55] In the vision of the Eagle of just kings, he sees that the Eagle *thinks* 'We' and 'Our', but it says 'I' and 'mine'.[56] Partnership has become a more intense unity. All this, with other incidents, leads on to the eventual knowing, in a flash, of the last great riddle when he sees the circle which is Christ painted with the image of man: 'I longed to know how the image consorts with the circle, and how it settles there'.[57] He had been given and he had repeated other answers; this, as far as he knew, he could not repeat. But it is the in-Godding of man that he sees.

It is along this way of experienced life that Beatrice accompanies her lover. In the *New Life* no-one had known what she willed; here it is clear—she wills to be for Dante what Dante needs. She has not to write the *Comedy*; she has two points—God and Dante. She lives, of course, like her lover, in and through the great

53 *Paradiso*, III. 77; see note 47 above.
54 *Paradiso*, III. 70–5, 82–5.
55 *Paradiso*, IX. 81, rendering two more neologisms by Dante.
56 *Paradiso*, XIX. 11–2.
57 *Paradiso*, XXXIII. 137–8.

Rose of blessed souls;[58] she is in no sense confined to Dante. But whatever Dante's need requires her to be, that, subject to God, she becomes. 'No-one in the world ever moved so quickly'[59] as she to help him in the beginning, so she told Virgil; and it is perhaps this to which Dante alludes when, in his last cry to her, he says 'O donna, in cui la mia speranza vige'—'O Lady, in whom my *hope* hath vigour . . . preserve thy magnificence in me'.[60] It is beyond even this after she has turned her eyes for the last time from him to God (so differently from that turning away of the eyes in the refused salutation in Florence), that Bernard, invoking the Blessed Virgin for Dante, says: 'Look how Beatrice, with how many of the blessed, clasp their hands to you'.[61] This is the last vision of her, imploring Deity through the maid-mother that Dante may be there, putting herself still at his disposal. 'O Beatrice, dear and tender guide!'[62]

But she also has been known. There are two great poetic moments in this movement of the two of them along the heavenly way which a little stand out. The first is when she is forgotten; the second is when she is seen. At the opening of the heaven of the doctors she exclaims to him: 'Ringrazia, ringrazia . . .' 'give thanks, give thanks to the Sun of the Angels'.[63] Dante is so moved by devotion at these words, and by desire for God, that for the first time in the whole history he forgets Beatrice altogether. 'Ma si se ne rise—'[64] she is so delighted at this that she laughs at the heavenly infidelity, and 'the splendour of her laughing eyes' catches his mind back

58 *Paradiso*, XXX. 117ff..
59 *Inferno*, II. 109.
60 *Paradiso*, XXXI. 79–90.
61 *Paradiso*, XXXIII. 38–9.
62 *Paradiso*, XXIII. 34.
63 *Paradiso*, X. 52–3.
64 'But she so smiled', *Paradiso*, X. 61.

from the vision (for which he is not yet ready)—to her? no, but to the glowing lights about him which are the great doctors of the Church. Even in the *Paradise* itself there are few more complex and intense poetic moments—and not many nearer an accurate image of actual experience. This too is a statement of what happens to the most ordinary people in love. A sudden apprehension of the Good takes place, and the very appearance of the admired form is at once forgotten in that and yet excites the mind to ardours of intellect. Such experiences may be brief but they are normal; they are the answer to the everlasting question whether Beatrice is Theology. She is, of course, Theology, but she is only Theology because she is Beatrice; unwomaned, she is also untheologized. 'The glorious and holy flesh'[65] is, in some sense, the exhibition of Theology incarnate; as, because of the Incarnation, it is and must be. And when all these mysteries are hinted, yet in Paradise they can be for awhile happily ignored; the joyous laughter of the Florentine at finding herself at last forgotten is as simple and natural as the surroundings are complex and supernatural. It is precisely a girl laughing in the City whom we hear.

The knowledge of the in-Godding proceeds. In the 23rd canto Dante sees his first glance of Christ triumphing among the redeemed—'one sun which set all burning'.[66] It is then that Beatrice calls to him to look at her indeed—in a voice different from that other invitation of the Earthly Paradise: 'Open thine eyes; look at what I am'—'riguarda'.[67] It is the cry uttered so often through the poem—'look, look well'; and he turns at it now, as she offers herself to his gaze—an offer worthy 'di tanto grato', of 'so great gratitude'.[68] This is the opposite of

---

65 *Paradiso,* XIV. 43. See note 52 above.

66 *Paradiso,* XXIII. 29.

67 *Purgatorio,* XXX. 73.

68 *Paradiso,* XXIII. 53. In the Temple Classics text Williams used this read 'grado'.

the false Thaïs flattery; infinite gratitude here is serious. He sees 'the sacred countenance made clear by the sacred smile',[69] the smile of one of the elect to another, but also the smile of Beatrice for Dante. It is, no doubt, a state of being far beyond the normal, and yet it is but the normal made infinitely profound: many young lovers must have known precisely 'the sacred countenance made clear by the sacred smile'. One can see it happening almost anywhere, in streets, at stations, in drawing-rooms; and even the protest of Beatrice which immediately follows is not alien. She who delights in being studied, whose great profit was to be studied, who carried so much love 'within her sacred eyes',[70] exclaims against it; she turns his attention elsewhere—'why does this face of mine so enamour you that you do not . . .' and so on; and she uses the word 'enamour', 'in-love', 'innamora'.[71] It is fitting that when, immediately afterwards, Dante is questioned by St. John, the apostle of love, he speaks of her again in the old manner; his own eyes, he says, 'were the gates where she entered with the fire in which I burn for ever'.[72]

It is impossible here to trace the diagram of the final movement. In the heaven which is pure light—'intellectual light full of love'[73]—he sees her at the last point of his power of speech of her; afterwards, directed by St. Bernard, he sees her in her place among the redeemed; he invokes her still to preserve him; they exchange their gaze. There follows the profound and mystical final substitution. The eyes of Beatrice have been the sign and means of ascent in experience; they have shown themselves to Dante and in a sense known heaven for Dante. But at the moment when 'Beatrice and all the blessed' implore

69 *Paradiso*, XXIII. 59–60.
70 *Purgatorio*, XXXI. 133.
71 *Paradiso*, XXIII. 70.
72 *Paradiso*, XXVI. 13–5.
73 *Paradiso*, XXX. 40.

the Divine Mother for him,[74] it is not her eyes that the poem means, though it may be her eyes also that the poem means. It is Mary's—'those eyes, loved and venerated by God'.[75] It is the mortal maternity of Godhead that is here expressed. But this also is not alien from the Way: what else had Beatrice seemed when she came after Joan in the mortal city?[76]

'Look well.' The whole poem is composed of variations on that *attention*. But I said at the beginning that the question here is whether this pattern, which is certainly a part of Dante's work, is a pattern to us; whether the diagram of romantic love which it presents, with every circumstance of tenderness and terror, is a diagram of value to us. People are still, it seems, 'falling in love', and a great many of them are falling in love after that manner, or so it still seems. It does not follow that they express it properly, or can so express it. The 'falling in love' may be of many kinds and many degrees; there may be more or less of vision, more or less of affection, more or less of appetite. None of these exclude another. I have already expressed my own belief that the vision is far more common than we who forget or betray or deny it understand. On the other hand, if this is so and if Dante is right, then if we neglect it we shall neglect, both for ourselves and for others, a Way of Sanctity. Marriage might be the most common exposition of the Way; as, no doubt, in many unknown homes it is. And if so high a potentiality lies in so many lovers' meetings, then those lovers might well be encouraged to believe in the Way and to become aware of what potentialities they hold. It is not to make us heavy and solemn; Eros need not for ever be on his knees to Agape; he has a right to his delights; they are a part of the Way. The division is not between the Eros of the flesh and the Agape of the

74 *Paradiso*, XXXIII. 38–9.
75 *Paradiso*, XXXIII. 40.
76 *Vita Nuova*, XXIV.

soul;[77] it is between the moment of love which sinks into hell
and the moment which rises to the in-Godding. Beatrice will,
no doubt, 'die'. But the eyes from which Love shot his earlier
arrows, the eyes which (St. John tells Dante) have the power to
clear his blindness, the eyes which are in heaven so full of love
for him, the eyes in which the two-natured Gryphon of Christ
is reflected, the eyes of the Florentine girl—there are the eyes
which in the end change only into the eyes of the Mother of
God.[78] This is the unique and lasting mystery of the Way.

---

77 'The difference may be shortly stated by saying that whereas in
    eros desire is the cause of love, in agape love is the cause of desire',
    Oliver Quick, *Doctrines of the Creed*, London 1938, 54.
78 *Purgatorio*, XXXI. 115–7, *Paradiso*, XXVI. 12, *Paradiso*, IV. 139–
    40, *Purgatorio*, XXXI. 120, *Paradiso*, XXXIII. 40.

5

Shakespeare's *Henry V*

With *Henry V*, therefore,[1] Shakespeare reached the climax of exterior life; it is at once a conclusion and a beginning. It is not primarily a patriotic play for the First Chorus knows nothing of patriotism nor of England, but only of *a Muse of fire which would ascend the brightest heaven of invention*[2] by discovering a challenge between mighty monarchies. Patriotism certainly keeps breaking in, but rather like the army itself: the mass behind Henry is dramatically an English mass, and as the play proceeds he becomes more and more an English king. So much must be allowed to the patriots; it is, however, for them to allow that he becomes something else and more as well, and it is in that something more that his peculiar strength lies.

Before defining that, however, and his own words I define it, it may be well to remark a few of the differences between *Henry V* and its precedent *Henry IV*. The newer manner of the

1 Despite the appearance of continuing from some previous material, this is an independent essay.
2 *Henry V*, opening.

blank verse itself is accentuated; it gains in speed. Less even than in *Henry IV* are there any involutions or adornments; its movements, like the action of the persons, admit of no delay. It has lost superfluity, though it has not yet gained analysis. No word blurs, but each word does not yet illuminate, as each was to illuminate in that later play of action and vision, *Antony and Cleopatra.* Here it is equivalent to the King's desire and the King's deed and equals the one with the other. But there is, at first, no variation between the King and other characters, as there is variation between the Prince and Hotspur and Falstaff in *Henry IV*: what the King is, he is, and the others are apart from him. In fact, the next differences between the two plays are (i) the omission of Hotspur, and (ii) the omission of Falstaff. It will be said that Hotspur is dead before *Henry IV* ends and Falstaff dies soon after *Henry V* begins. But whatever historical necessity or moral convenience compelled those two deaths, the result is to leave the stage free not only for King Henry himself, but for something else—for the development of the idea of honour. In *Henry IV* honour had been peculiarly the property of Hotspur, and it had seemed like being his property in a narrower sense. He had regarded it almost as if it were something he owned as he owned his armour, something that he could capture and possess.

> By heaven methinks it were an easy leap
> To pluck bright honour from the pale-faced moon,
> Or dive into the bottom of the deep,
> Where fathom-line could never touch the ground,
> And pluck up drowned honour by the locks;
> So he that doth redeem her thence might wear
> Without corrival all her dignities.
>
> *1 Henry IV*, I. 3. 201–7

Against this splendid and egotistical figure is the figure of Falstaff. Up to the last act of *2 Henry IV* the distinction of Falstaff had been that, though he may want a lot for his comfort, he does not need it for his complacency. Hotspur, without a sense of his own honour, feels himself deficient; it is why he rebels. Falstaff, without the same sense, feels himself free; it is why he runs away or fights as circumstances and his own common sense dictate. Henry V might have been made like either of them; in fact, he was made like neither. Neither Hotspur nor Falstaff could suit the Muse of fire or the brightest heaven. Honour must for Henry in his own play be something consonant with that brightness, and that invention discovered a phrase which made honour more than reputation—whether for possession or repudiation.

> And those that leave their valiant bones in France
> Dying like men, though buried in your dunghills,
> They shall be fam'd; for there the sun shall greet them
> And draw their honours reeking up to heaven
> Leaving their earthly parts to choke your clime.
> *Henry V*, IV. 3. 98–102

Their bodies are dead; their honours live, but not as fame upon earth. The heaven of invention is to suggest this other heaven; the honour of poetry is to show the honour of the spirit in challenge. It is a little reminiscent of *Lycidas*; where also Fame is transmuted into something pleasing to 'all-judging Jove'.[3] The honours which so live are the spirits and souls of the righteous—anyhow, of the righteous at Agincourt. It is to Henry that the identification is given, it is for him that honour is now a name for man's immortal part. If that venture of war which is the result of the challenge between two great worldly powers, two mighty monarchies, is defeated, this end at least is left to those who carry themselves well in that venture.

As far as the war itself is concerned, the play did not attempt any illusion. It put war 'in the round'. The causes of it are there; dynastic claims are the equivalent of the modern prestige

3 Milton, *Lycidas*, 82.

of governments. The force of the verse carries the sincerity of the intention, and the tennis-balls[4] are part of the cause of the war; that is, the other monarchy is also involved. Any insincerity is part of the way of things, but insufficient to cloud the glory of the change. In this sense Shakespeare threw over the diplomatic advice of the King in *Henry IV* as well as the martial egotism of Hotspur.

Besides the causes of war there is, in the first Harfleur scene, what a soldier-poet called 'Joy of Battle';[5] so, with a horrid faithfulness, in the second Harfleur scene, is the usual result of Joy of Battle. So, finally, in the field before Agincourt, is a kind of summing up. War is not so very much more dangerous than peace; one is almost as likely to be killed one way as the other. 'Every soldier's duty is the King's, but every subject's soul is his own',[6] which if he keep clean, it does not very much matter whether he lives or dies. Death is not all that important—to Henry (who in the play was going to fight), to the lords, to the army, and, as a consequence, to the citizens of Harfleur. The Duke of Burgundy's oration in the last Act[7] describes all the general advantages of peace, but it does not do more. Peace, as a general thing, is preferable to war, but life is pretty dangerous any way—pretty bloody, in every sense of the word—and a healthy male adult should be prepared for death at any moment. So what does it matter? It is not the modern view, but we are not Elizabethans, and our police are efficient.

Honour then—the capacity to challenge the world and to endure the result of challenge—is the state to be coveted.

---

4 The French ambassador insults the king by presenting him with tennis-balls in response to Henry's claim to the French crown, *Henry V*, I. 2. 258ff..

5 Julian Grenfell (1888–1915), 'Into battle'.

6 *Henry V*, IV. 1. 166.

7 *Henry V*, V. 2. 23ff..

But if it be a sin to covet honour,
I am the most offending soul alive.
Henry V, IV. 3. 28–9

Those lines come from the most famous of Henry's speeches. But there is another and much shorter and less famous speech which throws a stronger light on Henry. There had been a minor crisis—the conspiracy in the Second Act—before the great crisis of Agincourt. But as no one has the least interest in the Lord Scroop of Masham, and as no one can feel the King himself has had time to love him behind the scenes either in *Henry IV* or *Henry V*, the conspiracy fails to excite. We are left to listen to the King being merely vocal. When, however, the central crisis approached, Shakespeare had another way of being equivalent to it. This comes in the English camp by night before the battle, very soon after the greatest thing in the play, the sublime Fourth Chorus. In that Chorus a change had been presented as coming over the whole war. The venture had gone wrong, the challenge delivered to the world of the French had been accepted and that French world had trapped the English army and was on the point of destroying it. At the point of that pause the Fourth Chorus delivers its speech, describing the night, the gloom, and the danger. But its speech, if the words are literally followed, has two futures. The first is Agincourt; the second is the tragedies. There is not only a change in *Henry V*; there is a still darker change away from *Henry V*. The Muse of fire has been ascending her heaven—that is the poetry's own description of what it has been trying to do. But now it directly suggests that it is doing something quite different.

Now entertain conjecture of a time
When creeping murmur and the poring dark
Fills the wide vessel of the universe.
Henry V, IV. Prologue. 1–3

The word 'universe' means, certainly, earth and heaven in that darkness before the battle. But there seems no reason why it should not also mean 'universe' in the accepted sense, the whole world and the whole heaven, including the brightest heaven of poetry with which we began. It is all this which is beginning to be filled with creeping murmur and the poring dark. Poetry and (so to speak) life are being occupied by this universal noise and night. It is not yet so fixed; it is but a guess and a wonder. 'Now entertain conjecture—'. It is the prelude to all the plays that were to come.

From poetry thus conceiving of its own probable business, both locally at Agincourt and universally, and its future, two other enlargements follow. One concerns the English army; the other, the King.

The *Muse of Fire* is compelled to behold the army as 'so many horrid ghosts', and the description of the soldiers is that of men who are in the state she has described. It is an army but it is also humanity. To 'sit patiently and inly ruminate the morning's danger' is a situation familiar enough to us in peace as to them in war, if 'danger' also may be given a wider meaning than that of battle. Illness, unemployment, loneliness, these are the things that make sacrifices of 'the poor condemned English', that make them 'pining and pale'. It is among such a host of spectral images of mankind that the King moves, and the Chorus imagines him as their contrast and support: 'the royal captain of this ruined band'. It remains true, however, that the Chorus has to do this without having had, up to that point, much support from the play itself. Henry has been cheerful and efficient and warlike and friendly, but he has not suggested to us his capacity for being an almost supernatural 'little touch of Harry in the night'. The wider and the darker the night, the more that gleam shines. But why?[8]

8   All quotations in this paragraph and the next are from *Henry V*, IV Prologue, successively 28, 24–5, 22, 41, 47, 35–6, 39–40, 42, 43–4.

The cause follows. When the King appears he is speaking, more or less lightly, of the advantages which evil chances bring with them. It is not a particularly original remark, not a moment of 'great insight', and we need not perhaps suppose it is meant to be solemn or serious. It is in the next speech that the sudden difference between Henry and all the rest appears.

> 'Tis good for men to love their present pains
> Upon example; so the spirit is eas'd:
> And when the mind is quicken'd, out of doubt,
> The organs, though defunct and dead before,
> Break up their drowsy grave, and newly move
> With casted slough and fresh legerity.
> *Henry V*, IV. 1. 18–23

This is the centre of Henry's capacity. He 'loves' his present pains, and his spirit is therefore eased. He has rather more than accepted darkness, danger, defeat and death, and loves them. It is this which gives him a new quickening of the mind, new motions of the organs; it destroys sloth and the drowsy grave of usual life. It is this love and the resulting legerity of spirit which enable him to be what the Chorus describe, and what the rest of the Act accentuates.

> Upon his royal face there is no note
> How dread an army hath enrounded him;
> *Henry V*, IV. Prologue. 35–6

how can there be when he loves being enrounded?

> But freshly looks and overbears attaint
> With cheerful semblance and sweet majesty.
> *Henry V*, IV. Prologue. 39–40

It is precisely a description of what he has done within himself. Therefore every wretch 'plucks comfort from his looks', receiving the 'largess universal' from his 'liberal eye'—from the eased spirit, the quickened mind, the moving organs, which are the effect of his love for present pains.

Perhaps this also was something of the explanation of the dead Falstaff; perhaps Henry was more like his old acquaintance than he altogether knew. Only the word 'love' can hardly be used of Falstaff in any sense; it was by no accident or haste that Shakespeare could not show him in more 'love' than the odd possibility of lechery excites. He enjoyed his dilemmas in the sense that he enjoyed being equal to them, but Henry enjoys them because he is careless of them.

There is a distinction, and it lies in the fact that the King's spirit is 'honour' whereas Falstaff's is the rejection of 'honour'. It also lies in the fact that Falstaff does die when he cannot conquer 'the King's unkindness'.[9] If ever Falstaff's spirit was drawn reeking up to heaven, he would only enter it on his own terms, but Henry will enter it on Heaven's terms. It is Falstaff's greatness that we are delighted to feel heaven give way to him, Henry's that we are eased by his giving way to heaven. But the artistic difference is that there is no more to be done in the method of Falstaff—he is complete and final. He can be continually varied and repeated, but he cannot be developed. Henry is complete, but not final. For he, in whose honour there is no self-contradiction, could love his pains simply because there was nothing else to do except run away, and that the same honour forbade. The genius of Shakespeare proceeded, however, immediately to imagine an honour in which self-contradiction did passionately exist; it emerged as Brutus, and was set in front of a power which was more 'monstrous'[10] than that of the French army; he called that monstrosity Caesar,

9 Hostess (Mistress Quickly): 'the King has killed his heart', *Henry V*, II. 1. 84

10 Brutus calls the ghost of Caesar 'this monstrous apparition', *Julius Caesar*, IV. 3. 275.

and made another play out of those other conditions, in which the crisis is a more deeply interior thing, and the heaven of honour begins itself to be at odds.

Henry then has made of his crisis an exaltation of his experience; he has become gay. This gaiety—a 'modest'[11] gaiety, to take another adjective from the Chorus—lasts all through the Act. It lightens and saves the speech on ceremony; more especially, it illuminates the speech to Westmoreland. In view of the King's capacity the stress there may well be on the adjective rather than the substantive: 'We few, we *happy* few.'[12] His rejection of all those who have no stomach for the fight, his offer of crowns for convoy, is part of the same delight: so far as possible he will have no one there who does not love to be there. He makes jokes at the expense of the old men's 'tall stories' of the battle, and at the French demand for ransom. We are clean away from the solemn hero-king, and therefore much more aware of the Harry of the Chorus, and of the thing he is—the 'touch of Harry in the night'. The very last line of that scene—'how thou pleasest, God, dispose the day'—is not a prayer of resignation but a cry of complete carelessness. What does it matter what *happens*?

It is a legerity of spirit, the last legerity before the tragedies. Hamlet was to have a touch of it, but there is little else, in the greater figures, until, as from beyond a much greater distance, it is renewed by a phrase Kent uses of the Fool in *Lear*. Who, says a Gentleman on the moor, is with the King?

> None but the Fool, who labours to outjest
> His heart-struck injuries.
> *King Lear*, III. 1. 16–7

---

11 *Henry V*, IV. Prologue. 33.
12 *Henry V*, IV. 3. 60.

Henry's injuries are not heart-struck; he is no tragic figure. But he deserves more greatly than has perhaps always been allowed. The Muse, *entertaining conjecture* of a new and dreadful world, conjectured also a touch in the night, the thawing of fear, a royal captain of a ruined band, and conjectured the nature of the power of love and consequent lightness that thrills through the already poring dusk.

6

On the Poetry of
The Duchess Of Malfi

The Dutchesse of Malfy[1] is thought to have been written about
1613–14. Webster was then a man of thirty-four or so; he had
collaborated with other dramatists in various comedies and had
finished Marston's *Malcontent* for the stage in 1604. *The White
Divel* had been produced in 1608. By 1613–14 the Queen had
been dead ten years. It was twenty since Marlowe had been
stabbed at Deptford. Shakespeare was living in retirement at
Stratford, having finished *The Tempest* about a year earlier, and
being now (or a little before or after) engaged on his part of
Henry VIII. Jonson was still in his full powers; *The Alchemist*
had appeared some four years earlier, and *Bartholomew Fair*
was almost contemporary with the *Dutchesse.* Chapman had
finished most of his work. Tourneur's[2] *Revenger's Tragedy* had
been published in 1607. Fletcher, Massinger, and Ford were

---

1   In this essay Williams used F. L. Lucas's old spelling text of
    Webster's plays. References are to this edition.
2   This play is now generally attributed to Thomas Middleton.

still to do much work, Ford indeed practically all his. *The Changeling*[3] was to come in 1623. But the hour of that grand style had almost passed.

The *Dutchesse* is not on the level of *The White Divel*. It is almost permissible to see it as the very point of lessening of that tragic imagination which we call, roughly, Elizabethan. A phrase from the late and lonely terror of *The Changeling* may serve to mark the difference between the two periods, and perhaps even between *The White Divel* and the *Dutchesse*. In Middleton's play the murderer De Flores says to Beatrice who has employed him:

> Push! Flye not to your birth, but settle you
> In what the act has made you; y'are no more now.
> You must forget your parentage to me,
> Y'are the deeds creature, by that name
> You lost your first condition, and I challenge you,
> As peace and innocency has turn'd you out,
> And made you one with me.
> *The Changeling*, III. 4. 134–9

The phrase "You are the deed's creature" creates distinction between Elizabethan tragedies. It can be used as a measure; we can see by it what certain plays do and others do not do. *Hamlet* is hardly covered by it; the Prince, for good or evil, has no deed of which he can properly be called a creature; and Claudius is certainly not treated seriously as a creature of his. But *Macbeth* is precisely a play of this kind; it is in the fore-dooming, "We still have judgement here".[4] *The Revenger's Tragedy* is too wildly hideous a discord to bear any so composed an inevitability; it is its very character that anything may happen, and its effects are by no means so certainly within their causes. There is more

---

3 A collaborative play by Middleton and William Rowley. Williams overlooks Rowley's role.

4 *Macbeth*, I. 7. 8.

of that inevitable doom, that natural judgement, in *The White Divel*, though it is postponed till the last scene. Vittoria,[5] till then, remains magnificent; in the great act of the trial she dominates her deeds as she does her accusers. Her vitality thrives in her deeds, as Iago's does in his. Yet her dying phrase has something of that other sense:

> My soule, like to a ship in a black storme
> Is driven I know not whither.
> > *The White Divel*, V. 6. 248–9

Her creatureliness begins to be known to her. Flamineo, her brother, is spared even that, but then he is hardly of importance till his end. Webster found the greatest phrases for his people precisely as they approach their end. In Mr Eliot's lines

> He knew that thought clings round dead limbs
> Tightening its lusts and luxuries.
> > 'Whispers of Immortality'

Only something of this is true of the *Dutchesse*. It is necessary to decide in which of two ways to regard it. The first is to see it as mainly about the Duchess herself, with the last act forming a kind of—perhaps superfluous—epilogue. The second is to see the last act as a necessary part of the play; by which reading the Duchess becomes a less important figure and the title an accident. There is, I think, no real doubt which is preferable if possible. One should always begin by assuming that any play—indeed, any book—was meant to have the shape it has. It may prove impossible to maintain this, or one may be driven to judge the shape a bad shape. *Julius Caesar* has been an example of the difficulty; many readers have in fact come to believe that it has no outline or at best "a demd outline".[6] I think it has a shape, but

---

5 Vittoria Corombona, heroine of *The White Divel*.
6 'The two countesses had no outlines at all, and the dowager's was

The Celian Moment

this is no place to defend it. The *Dutchesse* certainly has a firmer exterior shape, if not so intense an imaginative unity. It has a shape, but it is hardly an organism except in its spasmodic and convulsive movements of great poetry.

In this it differs from its greater predecessor, *The White Divel*. There the Elizabethan convention of the daring, lecherous, and destructive spirit was given full play. The victims were inserted, and scarcely even that. But here much is made of the victims, and the destroyers scarcely begin to be important until their murder is achieved. Ferdinand has indeed something of life in the scene when he leaves the knife with his sister, but the Cardinal incarnates only by his fishpools; he is that at which the thing armed with a rake strikes upward, and he is a man only so. But sufficiently. There is hardly a better example of the way in which poetry creates characters, rather than (as we so habitually tend to think) that the characters independently exist and talk poetry. The imagined murderers of this play are, in a less moral and more purely dramatic sense than Middleton meant, "the deed's creatures". It lies somewhere between *The Changeling* and *The Revenger's Tragedy* in weight of significance; as it does between *The White Divel* and *The Devil's Law Case*[7] in chronological lessening of force. Webster's own genius was dissolving; I do not say it was less, but it was less determined. This is a play of mirrors, and the mirrors are curved, so that the figures are out of proportion. It does not perhaps matter much that the two brothers should seem to have no adequate motive for their murdered sister; we are used to that among the Elizabethans. Passion is continually seeking for a cause, as Iago's is. But it seems strange that Webster should have done no more for Antonio. The figure of the lover in him is thin and wavering; was it for this that the Duchess outraged her house by misalliance? He is a wraith by her, and wanders helplessly among things too high for him.

a demd outline', Charles Dickens, *Nicholas Nickleby,* Chapter 34.
7 A later play by Webster.

Bosola himself is something of a wraith. He says to Ferdinand: "I am your creature",[8] but this creatureliness is not active either in deeds or in apprehension. The present writer remembers, at an early age, reading this play among others in a great green volume called *British Dramatists*,[9] which ranged from Lyly to Shirley, and then seeing Bosola as an old crooked man, full of wicked malice, introducing madmen and murderers into the Duchess's chamber. It was the inaccurate reading of a boy, but it was a tribute to the general effect of the play that it should so transform the figure, and now I a little regret my earlier Bosola. This Melancholy, till the last act, does so little. He drifts in and out, helpless and "intelligencing"—that is, spying. It is all he is given to do. But it is astonishing that, in his first great scene with the Duchess, he should be given no more to say.

DUTCH. What are you? (*she turns suddenly to a Servant*)

SER. One that wishes you long life.

DUTCH. I would thou wert hang'd for the horrible curse
Thou hast given me: I shall shortly grow one
Of the miracles of pitty: I'll goe pray: No,
I'll goe curse:

BOS. Oh fye!

DUTCH. I could curse the Starres.

BOS. Oh fearefull!

DUTCH. And those three smyling seasons of the yeere
Into a Russian winter: nay the world
To its first Chaos.

8   *The Dutchesse of Malfy*, I. i. 313.
9   *The Works of the British Dramatists*, ed. John S. Keltie, Edinburgh 1870.

BOS. Looke you, the Starres shine still:

DUTCH. Oh, but you must remember, my curse hath a great
    way to goe:
Plagues, (that make lanes through largest families)
Consume them!

BOS. Fye lady!

DUTCH. Let them like tyrants
Never be remembred, but for the ill they have done:
Let all the zealous prayers of mortefied
Church-men forget them—

BOS. O uncharitable !

DUTCH. Let heaven, a little while, cease crowning Martirs
To punish them:
Goe, howle them this: and say I long to bleed—
"It is some mercy, when men kill with speed."
          The Dutchesse of Malfy, IV. 1. 108–33

We must suppose the interjections meant so, but it seems an
ill judgement, for even the Duchess's agony loses something of
itself in such a void.

As if Webster had been conscious of some weakness in Bosola
here, he concentrated more power on him in the next scene,
both in prose and verse; it is this which goes to make the death
of the Duchess terrible, for the madmen are only just gone and
the murderers are to come, and the Duchess is not allowed
to have her own moments uncommented. The scene must be
read in its place; but one phrase is worth remembering here.
When the Duchess exclaims, in six often-quoted words: "I am
Duchesse of *Malfy* still", Bosola counters, with awful lucidity,
in another six not so often quoted: "That makes thy sleepes so

broken."¹⁰ It is in this fourth act that the play, as we say, "comes to life"; that is, it becomes, after its own kind, credible; which again means that we are satisfied with the words, "felt in the blood and felt along the heart".¹¹ These revelations of the soul are at once thrilling and composing.

It is however Bosola who twice uses a word, which is once repeated by the Duchess, and (so repeated) seems to define the earlier part of the play; it is the word *dung*. The full sentence of which part was quoted above in the allusion to Bosola's creatureliness is:

> what's my place ?
> The Provisor-ship o' the horse? say then my corruption
> Grew out of horse-doong: I am your creature.
> *The Dutchesse of Malfy*, I. 1. 311–3

There is, so early, already a kind of corpse-light over this germinating dung. In the second act, when he brings the Duchess apricots in order to find out her condition, and she eats them, he says:

DUCH. Indeed I thank you: they are wondrous faire ones:
What an unskilfull fellow is our Gardiner!
We shall have none this moneth.

BOS. Will not your Grace pare them?

DUCH. No, they tast of muske (me thinkes) indeed they doe:

BOS. I know not: yet I wish your Grace had parde 'em:

DUCH. Why?

---

10 *Duchess of Malfi*, IV. 2. 139–40.
11 Wordsworth, *Tintern Abbey*, 29.

BOS. I forgot to tell you the knave Gardner,
(Onely to raise his profit by them the sooner)
Did ripen them in horse-doung.

DUCH. O you jest.

The Dutchesse of Malfy, II. 1. 141–51

This recurrence of the word at such a point of his "intelligenc-ing" increases the sense of a corruption nursing the good; so that the Duchess's own pregnancy has this spiritual evil about it. Then, in the fourth act, it occurs again, after the Duchess has seen the wax figures of her husband and children:

BOS. Looke you: here's the peece, from which 'twas ta'ne:
He doth present you this sad spectacle,
That now you know directly they are dead,
Hereafter you may (wisely) cease to grieve
For that which cannot be recovered.

DUCH. There is not betweene heaven, and earth one wish
I stay for after this: it wastes me more,
Then were't my picture, fashion'd out of wax,
Stucke with a magicall needle, and then buried
In some fowle dung-hill.

The Dutchesse of Malfy, IV. 1. 67–76

But now the dung and the corruption are one. Her phrase does but describe what is happening; the play is exactly her image buried in a dung-hill.

It is true that at first it is perhaps too well buried. In the apricot scene Bosola says of her: "How greedily she eats them!"[12] She is eating her bane, but that touch of greediness is also her bane, and has been. There are various opinions of her love-scenes. I

12 *The Dutchesse of Malfy*, II. i. 162.

have known women who rejected them from no prudery. She is no Miranda or Imogen; her love-scenes have no touch of illumination, and the fact that she is a widow and a mother is mentioned too often for it to be forgotten. Even if the scene of her wooing be accepted, her later passages of love with Antonio would be more delightful without the slight vulgarity. It is no question of mere sex. Vittoria—and Miranda and Imogen—had that. It is perhaps the presence of the waiting-maid Cariola that helps to spoil it, and Antonio's not very amusing trick on his wife.[13] The scene waits for Ferdinand to change it; but at least it is the Duchess whose words, when she so suddenly sees him, do so.

> Tis welcome:
> For know whether I am doomb'd to live or die,
> I can do both like a Prince.
> > *The Dutchesse of Malfy*, III. 2. 77–9

It is he who, speaking, of her and to her, uses words which re-define the corruption. He says

> Pursue thy wishes:
> And glory in them: there's in shame no comfort,
> But to be past all bounds, and sence of shame.
> > *The Dutchesse of Malfy*, III. 2. 92–4

But, in a sense beyond Ferdinand's, this is what he and the Cardinal, so far as they have been anything, have already always been. From now on, that lack of shame is open and exposed everywhere. The Duchess herself is not left quite free from it. When she is planning an escape, Bosola suggests that she shall pretend piety:

---

13 He and Cariola leave the room unobserved by the duchess so that she is left talking to herself but this allows her murderous brother Ferdinand to enter and threaten her.

BOS. Let me thinke:
I would wish your Grace, to faigne a Pilgrimage
To our Lady of *Loretto* (scarce seaven leagues
From faire *Ancona*)—so may you depart
Your Country, with more honour, and your flight
Will seeme a Princely progresse, retaining
Your usuall traine about you.

DUCH. Sir, your direction
Shall lead me, by the hand.

CAR. In my opinion,
She were better progresse to the bathes at *Leuca*,
Or go visit the *Spaw*
In *Germany*, for (if you will beleeve me)
I do not like this jesting with religion,
This faigned Pilgrimage.

DUCH. Thou art a superstitious foole,
Prepare us instantly for our departure.
                                 The Dutchesse of Malfy, III. 2. 352–68

It is true the pretence has been pressed on her, yet her answer
does her no good with us. Some momentary hesitation would
have saved all. It is however in the next scene that the persons
of Ferdinand and the Cardinal begin to stand out, when the
Cardinal "lifts up's nose", and "the Lord Ferdinand laughs".[14]
The murders are accomplished in the next act, and when
the bodies of the children are shown to Ferdinand his own
madness first begins to peep out:

             The death
Of young Wolffes, is never to be pittied.
                                 The Dutchesse of Malfy, IV. 2. 274–5

14 *The Dutchesse of Malfy*, III. 3. 63, 65.

He follows it with a borrowing from *The White Divel*:

> The Wolfe shall finde her Grave, and scrape it up:
> Not to devour the corpes, but to discover
> The horrid murther.
>> *The Dutchesse of Malfy*, IV. 2. 332–4

This is an echo of

> But keepe the wolfe far thence, that's foe to men,
> For with his nailes hee'l dig them up agen.
>> *The White Divel*, V. 4. 97–8

There are two or three such repetitions in this play, but generally of a lowered force. When Cariola says to the Duchess: "What thinke you of, Madam?" she answers:

> Of nothing:
> When I muse thus, I sleepe.
>> *The Dutchesse of Malfy*, IV. 2. 17–8

It is the changed: "Nothing; of nothing; leave thy idle questions" of Flamineo.[15] And the unfortunate and unnecessary Julia, dying by poison, says:

> I go,
> I know not whither.
>> *The Dutchesse of Malfy*, V. 2. 316

which is but an echo of Vittoria's cry.[16]

15 *The White Divel*, V. 6. 203.
16 My soule, like to a ship in a blacke storme,
    Is driven I know not whither.
>> *The White Divel*, V. 6. 248–9.

The word "echo" brings us back to its use in the *Dutchesse*, in the third scene of the fifth act. This is perhaps the most purely moving scene which the Duchess has. Her earthly greatness has ended—royalty and courage alike. She is not even required to make another entry as a ghost. Webster would not so enliven death; it would have too much broken up his bloody and again corrupting earth. She is not even an echo, but "there is an Eccho, (from the Dutchesse Grave)". Its first sound is the reverberation of "like death that we have"; its last, "Never see her more";[17] and it is almost the only beauty in those last acts of madness and death. Against it, the Cardinal's speech stands out, like hell against death, worse life against loss of life:

> CARD. I am puzzell'd in a question about hell:
> He saies, in hell, there's one materiall fire,
> And yet it shall not burne all men alike.
> Lay him by: How tedious is a guilty conscience!
> When I looke into the Fishponds, in my Garden,
> Me thinkes I see a thing, arm'd with a Rake
> That seemes to strike at me:
> > (*Enter Bosola and Servant bearing Antonio's body.*)
> Now? art thou come? thou look'st ghastly:
> There sits in thy face, some great determination,
> Mix'd with some feare.
> > *The Dutchesse of Malfy*, V. 5. 1–10

The end is, one might think, deliberately grotesque. Ferdinand's lycanthropy—say, his wolf-nature—has reached its height in the speech in V. 2.

> One met the Duke, 'bout midnight in a lane
> Behind St. *Markes* Church, with the leg of a man
> Upon his shoulder; and he howl'd fearefully:
> Said he was a Woolffe: onely the difference

17 *The Dutchesse of Malfy*, V. 3. stage direction, 21, 54.

Was, a Woolffes skinne was hairy on the out-side,
His on the In-side: bad them take their swords,
Rip up his flesh, and trie.

The Dutchesse of Malfy, V. 2. 14–20

After that the wantonness and assassinations are all but a
wearisomeness; the Echo sounds sadly and pitifully among
them, and then they begin again. At last, the death-scuffle
between the Cardinal, the mad Duke, and Bosola takes place
almost under the eyes of a deceived and amused Court. It is
proper. They die without many great phrases, the Cardinal
indeed without any. Ferdinand has his

I do account this world but a dog-kennell:
I will vault credit, and affect high pleasures,
Beyond death.

The Dutchesse of Malfy, V. 5. 85–7

But it is Bosola who sums up the play. It is almost like him; it
also holds its weary soul in its teeth. All the lords, and all love
and greatness, now

end in a little point, a kind of nothing.

The Dutchesse of Malfy, V. 5. 98

What then?

Oh this gloomy world,
In what a shadow, or deepe pit of darknesse,
Doth (womanish and fearefull) mankind live!

The Dutchesse of Malfy, V. 5. 124–6

7

The Poems of
Gerard Manley Hopkins

A good deal of attention has been paid to Gerard Hopkins's prosody, to his sprung-rhythms and logaoedic, his paeons and outrides; not so much has been spent on those habits, especially alliteration, to which English verse is more accustomed. Yet the alliteration so largely present in his poems is significant; especially if it be compared with that of another notable Victorian, Swinburne. It is of course a habit prevalent in all poets, but in general it is unintentionally disguised; the inexpert reader will not easily believe how much of it is in Shakespeare. But there have never been two poets who employed it more than Hopkins and Swinburne; and the astonishing thing about Swinburne is not its presence but its uselessness, as the admirable thing about Hopkins is not its presence but its use. In verse after verse words beginning with the same letter hurry to Swinburne's demand; and all that can really be felt about them is that they do begin with the same letter. There is thought in Swinburne—more than it has of late been the fashion to admit—but the diction does not help it. The two things run almost parallel, so separate are they; they often divide at the opening of a poem, and when they come together it is by chance. The result is that Swinburne alliteration will not usually stand close examination. Even the famous 'now folded in the flowerless fields of heaven'[1] leaves the reader with the feeling that 'flowerless' which might—there—have been so remarkable an epithet was as a matter of fact an accidental one. He was the child of the English vocabulary.

But Gerard Hopkins was not the child of vocabulary but of passion. And the unity of his passion is seen if we consider his alliteration: 'nor soul helps flesh more, now, than flesh helps soul'.[2] The first stanza of the first poem, after the early ones, *The Wreck of the Deutschland*, may serve as an example. It is enough to suggest here that the curious reader might separate such almost inevitable 'poetic' alliterations as 'Lord of the living' from those in which the intense apprehension of the subject provides two or more necessary words almost at the same time. 'Thou hast bound bones . . . fastened me flesh.' It is as if the imagination, seeking for expression, had found both verb and substantive at one rush, had begun almost to say them at once, and had separated them only because the intellect had reduced the original unity into divided but related sounds. A line like 'And cast by conscience out, spendsavour salt'[3] is one in which that intellect goes speeding to sound the full scope of the imaginative apprehension, and yet all the while to keep as close to its source as possible. It is true we cannot make haste when we are reading him, but that is what helps to make him difficult. The very race of the words and lines hurries on our emotion; our minds are left behind, not, as in

1 From the opening of Swinburne's *Atalanta in Calydon*, which Williams quotes again in the next paragraph:
   Maiden, and mistress of the months and stars
   Now folded in the flowerless fields of heaven.
2 Robert Browning *Rabbi ben Ezra*, stanza 12.
3 'The Candle Indoors'.

Swinburne, because they have to suspend their labour until it is wanted, but because they cannot work at a quick enough rate. 'Cast by conscience out' is not a phrase; it is a word. So is 'spendsavour salt'. Each is thought and spoken all at once; and this is largely (as it seems) the cause and (as it is) the effect of their alliteration. They are like words of which we remember the derivations; they present their unity and their elements at once.

The work of the intellect is in the choice of the words. One may compare again 'Maiden, and mistress of the months and stars' with 'Why, tears! is it? tears; such a melting, a madrigal start!'.[4] Madrigal is the last word expected, but it is justly chosen. So in 'Stigma, signal, cinquefoil token', 'lettering of the lamb's fleece', 'the gnarls of the nails' and many another. For all the art of the impulse and rush, 'the roll, the rise, the carol, the creation',[5] it is very evident that the original impulse was to most careful labour as well as to apparent carelessness. The manuscripts confirm this by their numerous alterations, deletions and alternative readings; they are what we might expect to find in the work-book of a good poet.

Of the same nature are his interior rhymes—as in 'The Lantern Out of Doors', 'heart wants, care haunts', 'first, fast, last friend', or the three last lines of the next poem;[6] and his mere repetitions—'and hurls for him, O half hurls earth for

4 *The Wreck of the Deutschland*, stanza 18. The next three quotations are also from this poem, stanzas 22 and 23.

5 'To R. B.', i.e. Robert Bridges.

6   Have lost that cheer and charm of earth's past prime:
    Our make and making break, are breaking, down
      To man's last dust, drain fast towards man's first slime.
        'The Sea and the Skylark'

him',[7] 'lay wrestling with (my God!) my God'.[8] Alliteration, repetition, interior rhyme, all do the same work: first, they persuade us of the existence of a vital and surprising poetic energy; second, they suspend our attention from any rest until the whole thing, whatever it may be, is said. Just as phrases which in other poets would be comfortably fashioned clauses are in him complex and compressed words, so poems which in others would have their rising and falling, their moments of importance and unimportance, are in him allowed no chance of having anything of the sort. They proceed, they ascend, they lift us (breathlessly and dazedly clinging) with them, and when at last they rest and we loose hold and totter away we are sometimes too concerned with our own bruises to understand exactly what the experience has been.

It is arguable that this is not the greatest kind of poetry; but it is also arguable that the greatest kind of poetry might easily arise out of this. Robert Bridges has said that he was, at the end, abandoning his theories. But his theories were only ways of explaining to himself his own poetic energy, and if he were abandoning them it was because that energy needed to spend no more time on explanation, because, that is, it was becoming perfectly adequate to its business, 'without superfluousness, without defect'.[9] While it was capable of producing lines like 'Or to-fro tender trambeams truckle at the eye',[10] it may very well have felt that it ought to do a certain amount of explanation, though it did not (as it could not) explain that. It is perfectly possible to smile at the line, but hardly possible to laugh; or only sympathetically, as at the wilder images of the metaphysicals, the extremer rhetoric of Marlowe, the more sedate elegances of Pope, the more prosaic moralities of the

7   'Hurrahing in Harvest'.
8   'Carrion Comfort'.
9   Coventry Patmore, 'Sing us one of the songs of Sion'.
10 'The Candle Indoors'.

Victorians, or the more morbid pedestrianisms of Thomas Hardy. Such things are the accidents of genius seriously engaged upon its own business, and not so apt as the observer to see how funny it looks.

The poet to whom we should most relate Gerard Hopkins, however, is perhaps none of these—not even the Metaphysicals nor the other Victorians—but Milton. The simultaneous consciousness of a controlled universe, and yet of division, conflict, and crises within that universe, is hardly so poignantly expressed in any other English poets than those two. Neither of them is primarily a mystic in his poetry, though Gerard Hopkins might easily have become one, or rather mysticism might very well have appeared in it. But such poems as 'The Blessed Virgin compared to the Air we Breathe' hardly suffice to mark his verse with that infrequent seal, any more than 'The Hound of Heaven' alone would seal Francis Thompson's. Both poets are on the verge of mystical vision, neither actually seem to express it. But if the sense of division and pain, of summons and effort, make mysticism, then Hopkins was a mystic, but then also Milton was. The suffering in 'Thou art indeed just, Lord' is related to the suffering of Milton's *Samson Agonistes*, though Milton, under the influence of an austerer religious tradition refused to 'contend'[11] with God as Gerard Hopkins was free to do. Both their imaginations nevertheless, felt the universe as divided both within them and without them, both realized single control in the universe; and both of them fashioned demands upon themselves and upon others out of what they held to be the nature of that control. This was the nature of their intellect.

Gerard Hopkins's experience of this is expressed largely in continual shocks of strength and beauty. Strength and beauty

---

11 'Thou art indeed just, Lord, if I contend | With thee; but, sir, so what I plead is just.'

are in all of the more assured poets; it is therefore on the word 'shocks' that emphasis must be laid. Any poet when he is not at his greatest is preparing us for his greatest; it is by that approach to him that we can discern the elements which go to make up the unity of his achievements. We can find in this poet's work the two elements which have been mentioned: (a) a passionate emotion which seems to try and utter all its words in one (b) a passionate intellect which is striving at once to recognize and explain both the singleness and division of the accepted universe. But to these must be added a passionate sense of the details of the world without[12] and the world within, a passionate consciousness of all kinds of experience. 'The Bugler's First Communion' is unsurpassed in its sense of the beauty of adolescence, as 'The Handsome Heart' or 'Brothers' of the beauty of childhood or 'Spring and Fall' of its sadness, as 'The Windhover' or 'The Starlight Night' are of the beauty of Nature, or certain of the sonnets of the extreme places of despair.

Yet perhaps, in the poems as we have them, the most recurrent vision seems to be that of some young and naked innocence existing dangerously poised among surrounding dangers—'the achieve of, the mastery of the thing!'.[13] Had he lived, those dangers and that poise might have been more fully analysed and expressed. As it is, his intellect, startled at the sight, breaks now into joy, now into inquiry, now into a terror of fearful expectation, but always into song. Other poets have sung about their intellectual exaltations, in none has the intellect itself been more the song than in Gerard Hopkins. In this he was unique among the Victorians but not because he was different

12 He is usually so exact in his outward detail that one slip which is certain to be remarked sooner or later by a student of such things may as well be noted here. It will be observed that the stranger in the most lovely 'Epithalamion'—admirable fellow!— in preparing to bathe, takes off his boots *last*. [CW]

13 'The Windhover'.

from them in kind—as they indeed were not different in kind from us or from their predecessors—only because his purely poetic energy was so much greater.

His poetic tricks, his mannerisms, his explorations in the technique of verse are not in the earlier poems and they are disappearing from the later. Had he lived, those tricks might have seemed to us no more than the incidental excitements of a developing genius. Since he did not live they will probably always occupy a disproportionate part of the attention given him. But that that attention must increase is already certain: poets will return to him as to a source not a channel of poetry; he is one who revivifies, not merely delights, equivalent genius. Much of his verse is described in that last line which in 'Felix Randal' brings in the outer world with such an overmastering noise of triumph over the spiritual meditation of the other lines; he himself at his poetry's 'grim forge, powerful amidst peers', fettled for the great gray drayhorse of the world 'his bright and battering sandal'. Some of his poems are precisely bright and battering sandals. But some again are like another line—'Some candle clear burns somewhere I come by'.[14] He is 'barbarous in beauty'.[15] But he is also 'sweet's sweeter ending'.[16] This again is the result of and the testimony to his poetic energy. He is integral to the beauty and storm without as to the beauty and storm within. But it will take a good deal of patience in us before we are integral to his own.

14 'The Candle Indoors'.
15 'Hurrahing in Harvest'.
16 'The Bugler's First Communion'.

8

Staring at Miracle:
A Vision by W. B. Yeats

Mr. Yeats's style imposes attention on his readers; no other living writer arouses so easily a sense of reverie moving into accurate power. But to express that attention properly would need more time than any review can take; and more than usually one must feel here the absurdity of trying to define patterns in other words than their own.

The book consists of "a revised and amplified version"[1] of an edition published in 1925.[2] A bibliographical note on all the contents would have been convenient. Those who know or possess the previous volume may still be glad, for Mr. Yeats has altered the exterior arrangements of his *Vision*, and what

1   Publisher's description.
2   This 1925 edition is known as *Vision A* by Yeats scholars, to distinguish it from the 1937 edition under review, which is known as *Vision B*. Quotations here are all from *Vision B*.

he calls the "unnatural story of an Arabian traveller"[3] is still peculiar to that edition. Certain poems are also reprinted to combine into a new volume. I have not yet been able to compare the two volumes, and must not, therefore, discuss the differences further.

The *Vision* itself is presented as a philosophical diagram of the nature of man and of the universe as known to man. It is said to have been communicated by invisible instructors, beginning with sentences delivered to Mrs. Yeats in automatic writing from 1917 to 1919. The method of communication was changed to speech in sleep during 1919. "Exposition in sleep came to an end in 1920, and I began an exhaustive study of some fifty copy-books of automatic script, and of a much smaller number of books recording what had come in sleep."[4] There had been interference at times which the communicating intelligences called Frustration or the Frustrators. Of the nature of this communication Mr. Yeats says that one intelligence said in the first month that "spirits do not tell a man what is true, but create such conditions, such a crisis of fate, that the man is compelled to listen to his Daimon." Mere spirits are "a reflection and a distortion"; reality is found by the Daimon in the Ghostly Self and "the blessed spirits must be sought within the self which is common to all".[5]

The symbolism of the Vision is geometrical, as all such imagery must be. In a sudden reminiscence Mr. Yeats alludes to the diagrams in Law's Boehme "where one lifts a flap of paper to

---

3   *A Vision*, 19. The 'unnatural story' is the Introduction 'by Owen Aherne', in *Vision A*. Owen Aherne was an alter ego of Yeats. A revised version appears in *Vision B* as 'Stories of Michael Robartes and his friends'.

4   *A Vision*, 17–8.

5   All three quotations from *A Vision*, 22.

discover both the human entrails and the starry heavens".[6] In another myth something of the same idea related the spiritual heavens and the womb of the mother of Galahad, and that last porphyry is like the porphyry room in Byzantium where the Emperors were born.[7] Here, however, it is a matter of cones or vortices, states of being struggling against each other, the "antithetical tincture" and the "primary tincture". "Within these cones move what are called the *Four Faculties*: *Will* and *Mask*, *Creative Mind* and *Body of Fate*."[8]

The movement of the Faculties covers "every possible movement of thought and of life,"[9] and these movements are marked by numbers corresponding to the phases of the moon. Mr. Yeats examines "the twenty-eight incarnations"[10] one by one, describing the kind of humanity observable in each and occasionally naming a few examples. Thus Phase Seventeen is distinguished as follows:

Will—The Daimonic Man
Mask (from Phase 3). *True*—Simplification through intensity.
False—Dispersal.
Creative Mind (from Phase 13). *True*—Creative imagination through *antithetical* emotion. *False*—Enforced self-realization.
Body of Fate (from Phase 27)—Enforced loss.
Examples: Dante, Shelley, Landor.[11]

Beside and beyond the Faculties are the Principles, *Husk*, *Passionate Body*, *Spirit*, and *Celestial Body*. "The wheel or cone

6   *A Vision*, 23–4.
7   A room in the imperial palace decorated with porphyry, hence 'born in the purple'.
8   *A Vision*, 71–3.
9   *A Vision*, 78.
10 *A Vision*, 105ff..
11 *A Vision*, 140–1.

of the *Faculties* may be considered to complete its movement between birth and death, that of the *Principles* to include the period between lives as well."[12] But even the full individual existence is only a part of the grand diagram; history also is measured by mathematics. Not the least fascinating part of the book is made of the 34 pages in which Mr. Yeats makes a pattern of Europe from 2000 B.c. to the present day, in a style which is dream, and in the dream diagram, and at that a diagram of greatness and terror.[13]

In a period when our cleverest men may write wisdom but do not habitually write English, the style is itself a refreshment. The sentence which refers to the Byzantium saints "staring at miracle"[14] is an example; another is that at which by chance I opened the book: "Love is created and preserved by intellectual analysis."[15] The intellect is so often nowadays regarded as merely destructive, or if constructive, then only in convenient and sterile things, that the phrase is near to being immediately rejected. But in fact it encourages the mind and more than the mind. Given the will, then the greater the analysis the greater the love, as has elsewhere been said: "Love is the chief art of knowledge and knowledge is the chief art of love."[16]

Yet perhaps to some minds in a different stage of thought, the

---

12 *A Vision*, 188.

13 *A Vision*, 267–300. The diagram is on 266.

14 'Both [Spengler] and I had symbolised a difference between Greek and Roman thought by comparing the blank or painted eyes of Greek statues with the pierced eyeballs of the Roman statues, both had described as an illustration of Roman character the naturalistic portrait heads screwed on to stock bodies, both had found the same meaning in the round bird-like eyes of Byzantine sculpture, though he or his translator had preferred "staring at infinity" to my "staring at miracle".' *A Vision*, 18.

15 *A Vision*, 275.

16 Williams, *He Came Down from Heaven*, Chapter V.

most thrilling sentence in the book is the one which Mr. Yeats quotes from Heraclitus. It is quoted in relation to the opposing cones: "dying each other's life, living each other's death."[17] If indeed the world is founded on an interchange so profound that we have not begun to glimpse it, such sentences for a moment illuminate the abyss. If so, it is the principle of some such exchange that must be sought before all national and international evils can be righted. "A civilization," Mr. Yeats says, "is a struggle to keep self-control."[18] Only by discovery of the principle of exchanged life can we keep our self-control by losing it, and without losing it we cannot keep it.

17 *A Vision*, 68 and again at 271. Yeats had used the phrase several times earlier, including in *Vision A*, 183, though there without the attribution to Heraclitus. See Introduction.

18 *A Vision*, 268.

9

Four Quartets: A Dialogue on Mr Eliot's poem

It is (said Eugenio, as he laid down *Little Gidding*) a most difficult poem to read aloud with a proper sensitiveness.

Nay, sir (answered Nicobar, in a youthful kindness of condescension), I protest you have done nobly, and Mr. Eliot, did he know, were indebted to you. A precise judge could not complain of anything beyond, here and there, somewhat of a greater rhetorical emphasis than the poem requires.

A fine thing, Nicobar (said Sophonisba, a little sharply), if you are to complain of rhetoric. It was you who, when you did us the kindness to read *The Dry Salvages*, seemed to attempt all the sounds of the sea.

Nicobar: Nay, madam (said he), I did but speak impartially. You are to consider that this last poem peculiarly removes itself from mortality, and is more like the cry of a strange bird flying over that sea from a coast beyond it than anything in the sea itself.[1] But I ask Eugenio's pardon if I have wronged him.

Sophonisba: What say you, Celia?

Celia had seemed in a study all this while, and now at first she said only:

Celia: Let us draw the curtains. There may be birds from beyond another sea tonight whose rhetoric would be less quiet than Nicobar approves. (And when this had been done, she went on.) But in truth, though I do not think Eugenio could have managed better, yet I am partly of Nicobar's mind.

At this they both smiled and flushed a little, being young and greatly affecting each other's person and judgement. But Sophonisba said:

Sophonisba: I do not know what you would have. Do you suppose one can express the soul by a monotone?

Celia: If Eugenio will pardon me, and I very well know that none of us three could more properly have satisfied the ear than he, I will say only that soliloquies from the heart's cloister are ever the most difficult poems to read aloud—perhaps

---

[1]   An echo of a passage in Yeats:
                    when I looked
          Where the dead drifted, I could see a bird
          Like a grey gull upon the breast of each.
          While I was looking they rose hurriedly,
          And after circling with strange cries awhile
          Flew westward
                    The Shadowy Waters (1906 version), 22–7

Williams greatly admired this poem, chose an epigraph from it for his own first volume, *The Silver Stair*, 1912, and discussed it in *Poetry at Present*, 1930, 63–4.

because they have in them something which contains a greater urgency even than poetry, but which is not poetry, or at least troubles us as if it were not. And while I listened to Eugenio, I was almost ashamed, as if I were eavesdropping, outside the door, to the murmurs of the prayers of some saint within.

Sophonisba: That is all very well, Celia, but you are to consider that Mr. Eliot would not wish to be taken for a saint, and if he has published his poem he has himself most certainly opened the door, so that we shall do him a double wrong to embarrass him with such comparisons.

Nicobar: Why, true, Sophonisba, but look at what you are saying. A poet may produce, *per accidens,*[2] an effect different from his purpose, and it would be hard to refuse to recognize an accent of the soul for fear of overpraising his own. There are examples of it in English verse. No one, to be sure, would call Patmore a saint, yet I have felt sometimes in the Odes which he wrote of Psyche[3] that I was intruding on a holy dispute for which I was not fit. Eugenio may perhaps tell us his mind now without thinking that Celia and I are to discredit his reading.

Eugenio: Nay, I hope we are all too wise to suppose that either verse or reading of verse is to be left free from judgement. And I think, if Celia will pardon me, that her modesty does but make her the fitter listener. It is said *He that hath ears, let him hear,*[4] and the undertones of our lord the Spirit are permissible for such intimate ears.

---

2 Accidentally; a scholastic term, contrasted with *per se*, essentially.
3 In his collection *To the Unknown Eros* Coventry Patmore included three poems on the subject of the fable of Eros and Psyche: 'Eros and Psyche', 'De natura Deorum' and 'Psyche's discontent'.
4 *Matthew* II. 15.

Four Quartets: *A Dialogue*

Sophonisba: Well, I think you are all making a great pother about a simple thing—

Celia and Nicobar: A simple thing! O Sophonisba![5]

Sophonisba: —and for my part, if we are to talk so, it was more a sermon than a prayer, and I will rather thank Mr. Eliot for an edifying instruction than pretend he has gone out of his pulpit into his oratory. I have heard my mother read as good an exhortation by the great Mr. Donne on a Sunday afternoon. But you young people do not read Donne.

Nicobar: Not read Donne! He was my pocket companion for long enough.

Sophonisba: Until Hopkins came in, I warrant. Poetry goes more by fashion than by favour. But some of your elders were familiar with ancient poets before we were taught them by Mr. Eliot's camp-followers. We had heard, too, of those exhortations, which of late are sieved in a pretty cullender of critical taste, so as to let through the dust of literature and keep out the gold nuggets of the soul. Only here it is strangely the dust which is prized and the nuggets thrown away.

Celia: Dear madam, we have heard you before now on your Dean. Would it please you to return to Mr. Eliot?

Sophonisba: Ay, child, you must ever have the new manners. You will be talking of him one day as I do now of Donne; nay, I have heard that some younger than you—to think of it!—speak of him already as of yesterday's load; and even those who were once his partisans suppose him to have flown off into hiding and clapped-to his wings in a church for want of other resting-place.

---

5 'O Sophonisba, Sophonisba O' was a notorious line in the play *Sophonisba* by James Thomson (1700–1748).

Eugenio: It is one of the strange diseases of our age—yours and mine, Sophonisba, for these young ones are clear of it—that so positive a mind should have been counted a negative. Those who supposed him disillusioned spoke perhaps wiser than they knew, for he stood from the beginning on a bare solidity. Few poets change much—and he less than some, except indeed in language. How did he put it? Reach me the poem, Nicobar.

> Trying to learn to use words, and every attempt
> Is a wholly new start, and a different kind of failure
> Because one has only learnt to get the better of words
> For the thing one no longer has to say, or the way in which
> One is no longer disposed to say it. And so each venture
> Is a new beginning, a raid on the inarticulate
> *East Coker*, V. 3–8

Poets, more than most, have their 'ends in their beginnings', their 'beginnings in their ends'.[6] Only by running very hard, as the Red Queen in Mr. Carroll's tale saw, can they so much as stay where they are.[7]

Celia: Is that moment, the moment of running and remaining, what he talks of in those passages of *Burnt Norton*? As

> . . . say that the end precedes the beginning,
> And the end and the beginning were always there
> Before the beginning and after the end.
> *Burnt Norton*, V. 10–12

Eugenio: The co-existence of the end and the beginning in the work of poets is perhaps an image of something more, and more general. Few poets have been able to go all their

---

6 *East Coker* begins 'In my beginning is my end' and ends 'In my end is my beginning'.

7 Lewis Carroll, *Through the Looking-Glass*, Chapter II.

distance; in any who have won to an end, and not to a mere
breaking-off, we may be aware that there is but one thing
said. I would not prophesy how noble or how lasting a poet
Mr. Eliot may prove to be, but, lesser or greater, he is one
who will have gone, it seems, all his distance. I speak only of
his art.

Celia: Might you not speak of more?

Eugenio: No, I would not dare it even of you with whom I
have had some close acquaintance, though I take pleasure to
think so privately. Nicobar may indeed write you a poem—and
he justly—admiring your spirit's perseverance, for at his age
such things are a joyous courtesy. But at mine I do you the
more honour to recognize your serious duty and the necessity
of your zeal. Or say I have talked with the apparition in our
poet's fourth poem.[8]

Sophonisba: Do you think, Eugenio, that that is the finest
passage?

Eugenio: It is, perhaps, for reasons, the most sustained towards
fineness. And you?

Sophonisba: I am no true judge of greatness. But I love better
the opening of *East Coker*—the lane and the dancing round the
bonfire and 'the time of the seasons and the constellations'.[9]
And the fourth movement of the other poem, *The Dry Salvages*,
which begins 'Lady, whose shrine stands on the promontory'.

Nicobar: It is lovely. And you, Celia?

Celia: I do not very well know. I think it is the manner of

8   *Little Gidding*, II. 25–96.
9   *East Coker*, I; the quoted line is 42.

incantation in each poem that I love best, and if Eugenio says that the last is the greatest I shall easily believe him. But for myself I think I love the other best, *Burnt Norton*, and all the birds and children, the flowers and sunflower, the footfalls echoing

> Down the passage which we did not take
> Towards the door we never opened
> Into the rose-garden.
>
> *Burnt Norton*, I. 12–14

Do not, dear madam, smile at me so tenderly. I am more than content not to have taken it. I have known more.

> After the kingfisher's wing
> Has answered light to light, and is silent, the light is still
> At the still point of the turning world.
>
> *Burnt Norton*, IV. 8–10

Nicobar: Celia!

Celia: O Nicobar!

Nicobar: But when he says

> that which is only living
> Can only die—
>
> *Burnt Norton*, V. 2–3

may we say that only that which does not live, as we mean living, will not die? Is everything else only 'the loud lament of the disconsolate chimera'?[10] How ridiculous and how right a phrase! Eugenio?

---

10 *Burnt Norton*, V. 22.

Eugenio: I would answer you if I were not afraid. But suppose that I am one of the foolish elders he talks of? Might I not, affirming it, offer you merely 'a receipt for deceit'?[11] It is your poem as much as mine.

Celia: I do not think you would deceive us unless we chose, and it would not then be for want of warning. He has taught us not to rely only on process. Read again, Nicobar; there, look!

Nicobar:

> We are only undeceived
> Of that which, deceiving, could no longer harm.
> *East Coker*, II. 37–8.

Sophonisba: It is a terrible saying.

Celia: I do not think it so terrible—even if it were true. But I am not quite sure that it is true, so long as one remembers that other saying—where is it?—about the action in the mind at the moment of death being that which should fructify in the lives of others, 'and the time of death is every moment'.[12]

Sophonisba: We are quoting our way through the poem.

Eugenio: It is the only valid way unless we were mastercritics. Or poets whose own poems might answer his.

Celia: Mr. Eliot's little body may by now be aweary of the great world of poets who do.

Nicobar: But, Eugenio, if we quote here and there and out of place, do we not alter the whole order, and make the poem

11 *East Coker*, II. 27.
12 *The Dry Salvages*, III. 33–7.

something different than it was? I could even play tricks with Celia's only Wordsworth so.

Eugenio: We can only remember to return always to the original; in that end is our beginning and in that beginning our end.[13] We must alter our order back again. For it is true we must say after every critic, however good, that

> There is only the fight to recover what has been lost.
> *East Coker*, V. 15

Nicobar: It will be a merry world in the grand art of poetry when every critic remembers that and so welcomes his next successor, and unloves his own particular. I cannot say that I see much business of the kind on foot at present.

Sophonisba: You said, Eugenio, that every poet who covered all his distance has said only one thing. Tell us, if you will, what you think Mr. Eliot has said.

Eugenio: I see it was a great rashness, and I must prepare to welcome you three my successors. But if you will have it in a poor phrase[14]—that you can only be a thing by becoming it.

Celia: May I remind you, Eugenio, that he has been called a learned, difficult, and obscure poet?

Eugenio: With reason—and even now with reason. I am not to remind you that the simplest things are obscure to most men and difficult to all. I have known Nicobar once or twice

---

13 This echoes the last and first lines of *East Coker*.
14 'Not to crack the wind of the poor phrase', Polonius in *Hamlet*, I. 3. 108.

expect a short cut, a metamorphosis as quick as Arachne's, or
as a more heavenly could I but think of a comparison. Virtue
and wisdom may sit with us at our feasts and walk with us on
our roads; they may even smile upon us so intimately that we
take them for our very hearts' masters, but all time is between
them and us unless we have given ourselves to the change, and
always the change. We may otherwise find on our death-day
how alien they are; or if before, when we are old enough to
know our harvest only deceit,

> only the knowledge of dead secrets
> Useless in the darkness into which we peer.
> *East Coker*, II. 29–30 (adapted)

I must alter the case to apply the words; he wrote 'they peered'.
Old men are like poets; few go the whole distance. It was
Bunyan, I think, who set a slumbering ground far beyond
battles and martyrdoms;[15] but the vigil must be for one knows
not what.

> I said to my soul, be still, and let the dark come upon you
> Which shall be the darkness of God. As, in a theatre,
> The lights are extinguished, for the scene to be changed
> With a hollow rumble of wings, with a movement of darkness
>   on darkness,
> And we know that the hills and the trees, the distant panorama
> And the bold imposing façade are all being rolled away—
> Or as, when an underground train, in the tube, stops too long
>   between stations
> And the conversation rises and slowly fades into silence
> And you see behind every face the mental emptiness deepen

---

15 'I saw then in my dream, that they went till they came into a
certain country, whose air naturally tended to make one drowsy,
if he came a stranger into it.' This was the Enchanted Ground,
Bunyan, *Pilgrim's Progress*, Part I, London, Folio Society, 2001,
127.

Leaving only the growing terror of nothing to think about;
Or when, under ether, the mind is conscious but conscious of
 nothing—
I said to my soul, be still, and wait without hope
For hope would be hope for the wrong thing; wait without love,
For love would be love of the wrong thing; there is yet faith
But the faith and the love and the hope are all in the waiting.
Wait without thought, for you are not ready for thought:
So the darkness shall be the light, and the stillness the dancing.
                    East Coker, III. 12–28

Celia: The stillness is the dancing. Movement is all within the stillness, that is true, and that is the difference between such a moment and all else. 'Love is itself unmoving.'[16] Is that 'the redemption of time'?[17]

Eugenio: What will you tell her, Sophonisba?

Sophonisba: I am not as oracular as you. But I know that the greatest moments are those whose movement is within them—yes, even all our little bodily movements.

Nicobar: 'The last apparent refuge, the safe shelter'.[18] Those moments are not shelters, because of the interior dance.

Sophonisba: Love is not a shelter.

Nicobar: You spoke, Eugenio, of the apparition in the fourth

16 *Burnt Norton*, V. 27.
17 'Redeeming the time because the days are evil', *Ephesians* 5.16. Cf. also:
    If all time is eternally present
    All time is unredeemable.
            Burnt Norton, I. 4–5.
18 Eliot, *The Family Reunion*, Part II, Scene 2. 309.

poem, or rather in the fourth part of the whole poem. Will you not discourse to us on it at more length?

Eugenio: I could say little that would make it more effective, and I might be too apt to catch the sad note of exposition, than which I can imagine nothing our poet—*poeta nostra*—would more dislike. We have not spoken of his allusions, which (if one knows them) enlarge his poem from within. But there is one here we must not altogether pass. 'What! are *you* here?'[19]—there is only one place in all Christendom where that cry was heard, and that was out of Christendom. Do you remember, Nicobar?

Nicobar: I had forgotten—till now. *'Siete voi qui, Ser Brunetto?'*[20] But why is the baked countenance of Brunetto Latini remembered here?

Eugenio: There is fire in the distance here—in 'three districts', as in that other place it fell from the dark skies; and here it is the time of 'the recurrent end of the unending',[21] much as the torments of Dante's hell in each moment become again recurrently unending. But we were not perhaps meant too closely to hunt out comparisons; or if, I am not the one to do it. Let us observe only how that terrible remembrance accentuates the cry, and how the dialogue between the poet and the apparition,

> a familiar compound ghost
> Both intimate and unidentifiable,
> *Little Gidding*, II. 42–3

19 *Little Gidding*, II. 45, echoing Dante, *Inferno*, XV. 30. See next note.
20 'Are you here, ser Brunetto?' Brunetto Latini was Dante's admired old mentor, whom Dante is distressed to find in Hell.
21 *Little Gidding*, II. 32 and 27; 'that other place', this part of hell where Dante finds Brunetto.

however different, is awfully undershaken by the Italian. The whole passage, correctly or incorrectly—or I will say wisely or unwisely—seems to me full of infernal reminiscence, though the English poet is ostensibly speaking of time ending here and not time unending there—and yet his words reverberate through the monotonous funnel of hell; indeed the funnel is here. Listen:

'Since our concern was speech, and speech impelled us
    To purify the dialect of the tribe
    And urge the mind to aftersight and foresight,
Let me disclose the gifts reserved for age
    To set a crown upon your lifetime's effort.
    First, the cold friction of expiring sense
Without enchantment, offering no promise
    But bitter tastelessness of shadow fruit
    As body and soul begin to fall asunder.
Second, the conscious impotence of rage
    At human folly, and the laceration
    Of laughter at what ceases to amuse.
And last, the rending pain of re-enactment
    Of all that you have done, and been; the shame
    Of motives late revealed, and the awareness
Of things ill done and done to others' harm
    Which once you took for exercise of virtue.
    Then fools' approval stings, and honour stains.
From wrong to wrong the exasperated spirit
    Proceeds, unless restored by that refining fire
    Where you must move in measure, like a dancer.'
The day was breaking. In the disfigured street
    He left me, with a kind of valediction,
    And faded on the blowing of the horn.
                  Little Gidding, II. 73–96

Is not that a proper summary of the dark journey from Styx

to Judecca?²² And is there anywhere a greater word for the deepening yet monotonous perpetuity of the lost than

> From wrong to wrong the exasperated spirit
> Proceeds?

Sophonisba: I have seen it said somewhere that the last line— 'And faded on the blowing of the horn'—has a relevance to 'Hamlet'—'It faded on the crowing of the cock'.²³

Eugenio: It may well be so, for there has been a reference to the 'refining fire' of that purgatory in which the ghost of the elder Hamlet dwelled. But you are also to remember that, below the sand where Brunetto Latini ran, there was indeed a horn:

> Ma io senti' sonare un alto corno.
> [But I heard a blast from a horn so loud]
> *Inferno*, XXXI. 12

And on that sounding Dante saw Nimrod, who held the horn and had destroyed speech, and the other giants and the last pit.

Sophonisba: You would say that that is what Mr. Eliot had in mind?

Eugenio: I would not take upon me to assert it. But I do not conceive that a mind pre-eminently stored with such learning is likely to have been unaware of such clear propinquities of meaning.

---

22 This is the journey made in the *Inferno*, though from the river Acheron in Canto II rather than from the river Styx which comes later, in Canto VII, to the bottom of Hell in Cantos XXXII–XXXIV.

23 *Hamlet*, I. 1. 157.

Nicobar: I remember your saying once, Eugenio, that this poet had, as it were, one moment which he put in many different lights, and I remember also that you compared the Eternal Footman in 'Prufrock'[24] to the Dweller on the Threshold[25] in a more ancient myth—

Sophonisba: What moment?

Eugenio: Alas, I have said so much that I do not clearly remember.

Celia: But I do. There was no particular kind of moment; it was then a moment in itself—any moment of time. And you quoted a line about the inability 'to force the moment to its crisis'. And I think, Eugenio, you rather hinted that you were waiting for Mr. Eliot to do so.

Eugenio: I hope, with a greater shyness than you seem to give me. But if—

Celia: Sir, you were as courteous as ever.

Eugenio: It is yours to keep me so. But 'force' for this poetry is too violent a word. It seems that there is a change; for now this crisis is within the moment. Most poets begin with man in a situation; presently man is himself the

---

24 'And I have seen the eternal Footman hold my coat, and snicker,' Eliot, *The Love Song of J. Alfred Prufrock*, 85.

25 An esoteric being introduced by the novelist Edward Bulwer-Lytton in his 1842 novel *Zanoni*: 'Know, at least, that all of us—the highest and the wisest—who have, in sober truth, passed beyond the threshold, have had, as our first fearful task, to master and subdue its grisly and appalling guardian.' The concept was taken up by theosophists who identified him with other mythical guardians such as Cerberus, the dragon killed by the angel Michael and so on.

situation; that is, in them, not an increase of knowledge but a mounting power of style. That is true of poetry, and more than poetry. The grace of time is to turn time into grace.[26]

> If all time is eternally present
> All time is unredeemable.
> *Burnt Norton*, I. 4–5

And again,

> The hint half guessed, the gift half understood, is Incarnation.
> *The Dry Salvages*, V. 32

Sophonisba: The Incarnation?

Eugenio: Do not let us say more than he. Our pious meditations may take what hints they choose, but let us keep them separate from our poetic. We wrong the poetry else, and we do not much help religion. Say only,

> With the drawing of this Love and the voice of this Calling.
> *Little Gidding*, V. 25

Celia: And all else only 'the loud voice of the disconsolate chimera'.[27]

Eugenio: Either that or the end of his 'Ash-Wednesday'—'And

---

26 Cf. from *Taliessin through Logres*:
   Time's president and precedent, grace ungrieved,
   floating through gold-leaved lime or banked behind beech
   to opaque green, through each membraned and tissued experience
   smites in simultaneity to times various veined.
   'The Departure of Merlin', 45–8.

27 *Burnt Norton*, V. 22.

let my cry come unto Thee'.[28] Leave it; we shall not end better than with those two lines.

Celia: Shall we go, Nicobar? Good night, Sophonisba; good night, Eugenio; and may the wish not be the voice of the chimera, but come with the cry where the cry comes. Good night again, and blessings.[29]

---

28 *Ash Wednesday*, final line, quoting the standard response in the *Book of Common Prayer* to the invocation: 'O Lord, hear my prayer', itself quoting Psalm 102, King James Bible version.

29 The repeated 'Good night' echoes Ophelia in *Hamlet*, IV. 5. 71, itself echoed by Eliot, *The Waste Land*, II. 170–2.

10

Ourselves and the Revolution

The impact of Russia on what is called the West but what is, in fact, for most of us, more immediately Britain, is a business which may easily become more difficult and more serious than at present it seems. It is to be assumed that the war effort now being made will result in victory, and that any views that stretch beyond such a victory are so occasional and long-term as to be almost cloudy. At the moment our gaze is, and ought to be, concentrated on provisions of war. At the same time it can do no harm to take a glance sometimes at the Power to whom we have the honour to send those provisions.

On the famous Sunday when the invasion of Russia took place, I happened to hear Mr. Churchill's speech from the lounge of an Oxford hotel.[1] There is no question of attack on the other

---

1 Hitler's invasion of Russia, Operation Barbarossa, began on Sunday 22 June 1941. Churchill condemned it in a radio broadcast that day and offered help to the Soviet Union.

people in the lounge—most of whom were probably, and many of whom certainly, were engaged in the war effort—if I admit that as the Prime Minister made plain that Russia and we were now, by the force of events, strong allies, a certain sense of the strangeness of the event pervaded one. It was ominous—not in any way meaning evil-ominous. Something was certainly happening which was, after we had won, going to make a difference. What did we, in that lounge, *know* of Russia? What did Russia *know* of us, in that lounge? A number of books, some music, a little history, occasional personal acquaintances, some notion (if we belonged to certain groups) of religious traditions, and general rather vague and probably inaccurate opinions about our separate political systems. It seemed we were likely, one way or another, to find out more.

Russia . . . the Orthodox . . . the Czar . . . Lenin . . . Karl Marx . . . the Bolsheviks; what did that revolution mean? It meant, very largely, the stomach. It meant, our cultural and religious experts assured us, a rather unscientific materialism; so, no doubt, it might. It meant persecution and cruelty; so, no doubt, it did. The Jacquerie,[2] the Revolution, had meant the same—less perhaps, perhaps more. One's haphazard mind could not tell. But the one thing it did seem to mean was the insistence on the desirability of a full stomach.

Anyone who has ever been in serious danger of not having a full stomach, anyone (that is to say) who has seen a serious possibility of being indefinitely without food or shelter, except by—whatever the State's methods now are, has undergone a quite particular and valuable experience. And no one who has not had that experience ought to be allowed, in social articles, to use the word "insecurity". Insecurity means that you do not know how you are to pay for food and shelter, either for yourself

2   A popular rising against the nobility in France in 1358, so named because the common people wore a garment known as a *jacque*.

or your family. It is, outside extreme physical pain, the worst experience of man; broken hearts are nothing to it. All our lives, we know, are insecure. But that general statement is one thing, and the experience of an insecurity which is unavoidable and irremediable is quite another. It may encourage us to faith in God; it may not. On the whole, so far as one can observe, it does not; and still more as far as one can judge one's own experience, on the whole it does not. Our Lord foresaw that the cares as well as the riches of this world were apt to destroy the Kingdom of heaven that is within. He did not there distinguish between the cares of the poor and the cares of the rich.[3]

I do not know in what particular way the Russian people experienced insecurity. But I know very well in what way the English did. There expanded over them a sky of iron from which the faces of their rulers looked down, uttering such phrases as: "There must always be a margin of unemployment," "the distressed areas," "social reform."[4] To know that from the skies, however sympathetically, is not to know it from below. One hung—a child—over the abyss of being "thrown on the streets," whatever that meant: by the thin thread that might be cut by one's employer's dislike, by some mere chance, or even by the Revolution itself. "There are," said Chesterton long since, "three kinds of men in England—fools, knaves and revolutionaries."[5] But even to be a revolutionary demands courage—a full stomach or an empty. Our stomachs were always queasy.

3   The parable of the sower, *Matthew* 13.3–23, particularly 22, with parallels in *Mark* and *Luke*.

4   The 1930s were a time of great hardship in much of England, particularly in the North, because the decline of manufacturing industries led to unemployment and poverty.

5   'By Morris's time and ever since, England has been divided into three classes: Knaves, Fools and Revolutionists', G. K. Chesterton, *The Victorian Age in Literature*, 1913, Chapter 4.

When, in 1917, the Russian Revolution began, it seemed to some of us as if for good or evil Earth itself had spoken. Those immense masses had done something—what we did not know then, and do not very well know now. I have myself heard the late Rev. Lord William Cecil,[6] preaching in St. Alban's Cathedral, say that his father, Lord Salisbury, was reluctant to interfere with the social system—because of his submission to the Will of God. Salisbury would no doubt have put it less crudely, but certainly the Will of God had, from what those voices of our rulers said, got curiously mixed up with that iron sky. In Russia it seemed that Earth shouted against it, and it broke. I am not saying that, even then, we thought it was altogether a pleasant shout. I am not saying that we thought the Russian revolutionaries were agreeable, or that we became Marxists or Communists. It was not so much that our minds were instructed as that our stomachs were queasy. But there has lingered—all these twenty-five years—a half-hope that the Revolution would not fail.

There is nothing more clear than that the Church was, still is, and for a long time will be, identified by the emotions of many of the people with what seemed to us a gross, careless, and cruel social rule, the rule that pushed us to or left us on the edge of the abyss. It is untrue? Certainly; but we are not to be blamed for the untruth. It was pure good luck that, for some of us, the great traditions and the Faith itself, were saved from confusion with the harsh society that accompanied it. But the result is that the jargons of both sides seem to us now equally untrue. Our hearts and brains are both divided. We are still Liberals at heart; we still believe in liberty; we even try to practise it. But when we hear liberty praised at the expense of security, we remember those queasy stomachs.

6 Lord William Cecil (1863–1936) was Bishop of Exeter. He was the second son of Lord Salisbury (1830–1903), who was Prime Minister several times.

I have seen the Hammer and Sickle fly over Oxford.[7] I have
heard the word *Red*, so lately used as a synonym for all that
was horrid, used now as a synonym for all that is noble. The
masses that are working and fighting in Russia are men and
women of full stomachs, and even (in the ancient sense) of a
high stomach. The whole, and only, question is whether we
can keep liberty and yet create security. The great thing that
is, when this is written, still advancing across those plains and
may (if it is ultimately victorious) advance a very great deal
nearer us has, it seems, created security, by some loss of liberty.
The extremely serious question is whether we are going to
be able to talk their language or they ours. If the languages
are still to be distinct and mutually incomprehensible I do
not much doubt which will survive. It will not be ours. But I
do not think that single survival is the only possibility. Even
between America and Russia the English may still have a
place. But then we must *mean* both freedom and security; we
must speak of tradition and of the Revolution; and we must
speak freshly and credibly.

We have a precedent. In matters of religion the East and
the West have, a little, "got together."[8] The very astonishing
movements towards a sense of the desirability of unity were
wholly unpredicted. No doubt these are partly due to a
natural fear. Virtue, however, can arise from sin, so only that
the virtue be honestly followed. If the supernatural life opens
such prospects, may not the natural? Yes, if we can meet with
really living hearts. The Orthodox East has taught us; the
Revolutionary East must teach us. What? Natural union in the
security of all. It is agreed by all Christians that we must not

7   The hammer and sickle flag, symbolizing the alliance of industrial
    workers and peasants, was the flag of the Soviet Union.
8   In 1937, as a result of various ecumenical initiatives, Christian
    leaders agreed to found a World Council of Churches, though
    the war delayed its inauguration until 1948.

expect here a sinless world. But it is also agreed that that—and that only—is what we must every moment aim at. We must not, we are told, and properly told (only so eagerly and darkly), expect "heaven upon earth." No? No. But all the same we are to pray that God's will "may be done in earth as it is in heaven."[9] The second phrase is sometimes instinctively ignored; what is it there, but pure and full delight in all from all through Him? What else should it be here? It was He who gave us the prayer; not we ourselves.[10]

What, then, is our business? Platitudes, but with a new voice. We are, even physically, members one of another. The Russians, it seems, have always strongly felt that; their virtues and their follies have that in them. The Church meant it; their Revolution meant it—in one sense or another. We have had our own virtues; we do not, on the whole, much want to interfere with other people; and we do, on the whole, wish other people so to behave that we shall not feel bound to interfere with them. But that reluctance to interfere has its dangers. Our very imagination of liberty has, to some extent, led us into allowing insecurity. It was easier not to interfere with our immediate neighbour than to prevent him ill-treating us. Besides, a scepticism lay in our hearts; we, no more than some of the Russians, believed that man could ever be happy. The new Government of Russia did its best to ensure that at least he should not be hungry. They created a totalitarian State for that purpose—whether they succeeded or not. They insisted that men should be members one of another, or die.[11]

9 From the Lord's Prayer in the version in the *Book of Common Prayer*, based on *Matthew* 6.9ff..

10 'Be ye sure that the Lord he is God: it is he that hath made us, and not we ourselves; we are his people, and the sheep of his pasture.' Psalm 100. 2, *Book of Common Prayer*, where it is also an alternative Canticle to *Benedictus* in Morning Prayer.

11 'We must love one another or die.' W. H. Auden, *September 1, 1939*, first collected in *Another Time*, 1940.

It was perhaps a harsh stress on a natural fact, but it did not alter the fact.

It is that fact which we shall have to believe, in mind and blood, if we are going to be able to talk to the Revolution. We have believed it for war; can we believe it for peace? I think we can; at least, I hope so. We have had, in the last year or two, to consider in a degree we never thought to consider, the permanent defeat of England. We are now invited to consider the permanent life of England. The Russians of late have been (one gathers) reasonably fed but not altogether free; we have been reasonably free, but not anything like enough fed. The metaphor of food may be pressed; we must learn to consume and be consumed, to eat and to be eaten. The principle of supernatural life, as we hold it, is the principle of natural life; the stomach is, in this sense, its image. The great social maxim—"from each according to his power; to each according to his need"[12]—is its definition. This is common; let us take it so. If the Revolution and the English can indeed, in that happy sense, mutually "eat and be eaten," Europe might—one does not know, but Europe might—be noble, fed, and free, even yet.

12 Best known from Karl Marx, *Critique of the Gotha Programme*, 1875, though several earlier writers also used the phrase and there is a similar sentiment in the New Testament, *Acts* 4.32–5.

Made in the USA
Las Vegas, NV
11 October 2024

96695624R00089